White Awareness

HANDBOOK FOR

White Awareness

ANTI-RACISM TRAINING

Second Edition

By Judith H. Katz

University of Oklahoma Press : Norman

This book is published with the generous assistance of The McCasland Foundation, Duncan, Oklahoma.

Library of Congress Cataloging-in-Publication Data

Katz, Judith H., 1950–
    White awareness: handbook for anti-racism training / Judith H. Katz.—2nd ed.
        p. cm.
    Includes bibliographical references and index.
    ISBN 0-8061-3560-3 (pbk.: alk. paper)
        1. Racism. 2. Race discrimination—Psychological aspects. 3. Caucasian race. 4. Group relations training. 5. Race awareness. 6. Racism—United States. I. Title.

HT1523.K37 2003
305.8—dc21

2003044751

The paper in this book meets the guidelines for permanence and durability of the Committee on Production Guidelines for Book Longevity of the Council on Library Resources. ∞

1 2 3 4 5 6 7 8 9 10

Contents

Preface

When I first wrote this book, I hoped it would be a useful tool for challenging racism, but I never imagined it would continue to be necessary more than two decades later. That it is still in print and still widely used speaks both good and ill about those intervening years. The anti-racism movement has grown and gained momentum—but so has the need for it.

Racism is still very much with us today, and it has taken some new forms. Although overt racism is still very present (we see it in racial profiling, acts of violence, and other obvious manifestations), a subtler form has emerged in the attitudes, words, and behaviors of many people who would never consider themselves racist. Indeed, most white people have such a negative association with the word *racism* that we are loath to identify with it at all. And yet, racism is still pervasive. Uncovering subtle racism is the critical frontier for anti-racism training today, and I am pleased to think that the exercises in this book can make real progress in addressing it.

Subtle racism is often rooted in the pervasiveness of white culture, which for many of us is so automatic and taken for granted that we do not see it. We tend to think of our way as *the* way rather than as one cultural perspective. White privilege, white power, and white ownership reside in this assumption. They are what we have to uncover to raise our awareness—our white awareness—of racism and how it functions in our communities, our institutions, and ourselves. Only then can we become agents of change with and allies to people of color.

For me, becoming aware of racism and owning my whiteness has been a long process, one that I have often fought and rejected. It is a process that has been marked by introspection, confrontation, anger, frustration, confusion, shame, and guilt, on the one hand, and the joy of discovering and owning my identity and finding a new sense of personal freedom, on the other.

The roots of this process—and this book—go back to my early childhood. My Jewish parents were forced to leave Germany during World War II. They settled in New York City, where I grew up. Often they discussed their concerns about equality and fairness with me as a young child. Their own experiences with oppression—being beaten and in fear of their lives because of who they were and the lasting impact of this—became evident to me as I grew. This awareness became an important foundation for my later exploration of racism.

It was not until my college years in the late 1960s and early 1970s, however, that racism had a personal impact on my life. I became involved with what was then called the "human relations movement" and sensitivity training. In this forum I became introspective and began to examine some of my values and behaviors. My interactions with people of color—particularly students and professors—led me to see other perspectives and acknowledge that racism does indeed exist.

A real turning point for me came during a six-day residential seminar. The participant population was 85 percent Puerto Rican and black and 15 percent white. For the first time in my life I found myself in a situation that was not white or Jewish dominated. I was confronted both subtly and overtly with my whiteness, my assumptions, and my values. No longer in the majority, I felt the need to seek out the support of other white people—to eat, talk, socialize, and identify with them. I found myself feeling defensive about my whiteness and guilty and hurt because I was labeled the oppressor.

When I shared this with the group, people understood, but they also challenged me. My guilt did not fix any problems, they said, nor was it healthy for me. It was essentially a self-indulgent way to use up my energy. The real issue was not whether I was concerned about addressing racism but what I had done to challenge it. What *action* had I taken? By not acting, I supported and perpetuated racism. I was told, "Don't sit here telling us what you would like to do—do it! And make sure you take that action where it needs to be taken—to the white community, where the problem is."

Since then the question, What have you done? has been the motivating force in my search to uncover racism within myself and to actively combat racism. This training program is an attempt to answer that question and serves as a partial response to the need to find a meaningful way to help create change in the white community.

This program developed out of my work with sensitivity training groups. After participating in many black-white "T-groups" (training groups), I began to realize that all too often whites would ask people of color to discuss their experiences with racism and oppression so that whites could learn firsthand about the realities of racism. Whites would often then refute the validity of those experiences, insist that we experienced the same treatment, accuse people of color of being "too sensitive," or feel guilty about being white. Whites often left the experience with our prejudices intact, or feeling a great deal of anxiety about our whiteness. Blacks often left feeling angry or hopeless. They also felt used: the burden of educating whites had been placed on them.

Along with colleagues at the University of Massachusetts, Amherst, in 1972 I began to facilitate white-on-white groups as a way to address white people's role and responsibility in supporting and perpetuating racism. Over the succeeding years this process crystallized into the systematic conceptual and experiential format presented in this book, a book designed to be a tool for facilitators working with an all-white group. White-on-white training is not enough in itself; cross-race education is essential too. White-on-white groups, though, offer a safe and focused forum in which whites can learn and share without becoming defensive or paralyzed by guilt. The question, of course, is what happens after they complete the training? The real test of effectiveness lies in taking action.

Over the years I have conducted numerous workshops for other white people to help them confront and address racism. I have also worked for twenty years as an organizational change agent and consultant, work that has taken me deep inside organizations where I see issues of racism—and other *isms*—play themselves out in various ways. I have learned that white people often do not recognize the power we wield until it is pointed out to us. This applies equally to the power we have to oppress and the power we have to effect change.

This book is, therefore, designed for white people. It is a means to help us break out of the oppressor role, to take a deeper look at the many impacts of racism on people of color and whites, and to take steps toward change and being more fully human.

Many of the exercises and discussions here focus on black-white relations. This is not to imply that other people of color in the United States do not experience the oppression of racism. I have focused on black-white relations as one pervasive example. It would be useful to discuss the effects of racism on other people of color, and I recommend that you do so. Facilitators should be aware of both the similarities of the effects of racism on all these groups and the unique ramifications of oppression and racism in the United States on each group.

Today there is much to celebrate in the fight against racism. People of color are more visible than ever before, and in just about every area of U.S. society they enjoy more power and more opportunity than ever before. This progress, however, has not made us immune to racism; it has given rise to new, more virulent strains. White people must continue to do the hard work required to promote a more equal and inclusive society. It starts with self-examination, and if this book does nothing else, I hope it opens dialogue among whites about racism and our potential role for change at the individual, institutional, and cultural levels. Too often today it seems many whites "don't want to go there" for fear the conversation will lead someplace unsafe or hopeless.

Our self-examination as white people may be uncomfortable at times, but it should never feel unsafe or hopeless. As I wrote in my original preface in 1978:

> It is my goal that we may ultimately find comfort in our move toward liberation, no matter how painful the self-probing may be. As whites we must deal with our racism so that all people may be free. It is through this process of self-examination, change, and action that we will someday liberate our society and ourselves. (vii–viii)

That message is as true now as it was then.

I would like to express sincere gratitude to the many friends and colleagues—too numerous to name here—who have contributed to the preparation of this book. Their faith, wisdom, support, and encouragement have played a crucial role in my life and my development as a change agent. A few require individual mention.

First, a broad thank you to the pioneers in this field whose work has moved us all forward. In reviewing the manuscript for this edition, I was careful to leave some citations unchanged, to honor the contributions of those who came before and to help the reader understand that there is a history, a context, and a continuity to anti-racism work.

I am deeply grateful to my friend and colleague Allen Ivey, who has remained a strong supporter and role model all these years. Bailey Jackson is one of the preeminent thinkers for conceptualizing and confronting racism in our society; I thank him for his friendship and for his leadership in this field. George Henderson, Chair of the Human Relations Department at the University of Oklahoma, has remained over time and distance a champion for change. Jeff Hitchcock is doing important and exciting work at the Center for the Study of White American Culture, Inc., and has become a wonderful colleague who made important contributions in updating this edition. Edie Seashore has been a brilliant mentor, a rigorous supporter, and a loving friend throughout my career.

I am appreciative of all the support and help I have received from members of The Kaleel Jamison Consulting Group, Inc. In particular, I thank Mickey Bradley for his help in rewriting parts of this book, Caryn Cook for her unwavering support, and Liz Bryant for helping to move the book to its completion.

Frederick A. Miller, my business partner and CEO of The Kaleel Jamison Consulting Group, Inc., has coached, loved, supported, and challenged my growth and thinking for many years. As an African American man, he has been a pioneer in the field of addressing oppression and modeling change. Through our work together over the years I have deepened my understanding of leveraging our differences as we work together for change. I could not imagine a better business partner. Thank you, Fred, as always.

And most important, I thank David B. Levine, my life partner and the man to whom I am married, who has supported me in becoming the change agent I am today and who has shown me how to be both aggressive as a change agent in the world and loving in my life. Through our life together I continue to garner the strength and courage to live my values passionately and fully.

JUDITH H. KATZ, ED.D.

Washington, D.C.

PART ONE Introduction

CHAPTER 1

Racism Today

We live in an age of self-examination. During the past several decades, U.S. culture has in many ways opened to allow exploration—through therapy, through dialogue, through mass communication and mass media—of areas formerly deemed too sensitive to discuss in public. On issues ranging from women's equality to lesbian, gay, and bisexual civil rights, from religion to political ideologies, there is more open dialogue and a variety of forums for the expression of a range of opinions. These conversations are being held in schoolrooms, lecture halls, corporate boardrooms, and television studios. They extend into all areas of contemporary society.

Despite these open discussions of sensitive issues, our conversation on race and racism seems nonexistent or—where it does exist—is mired in misinformation and miscommunication. One reason for this is our tendency to avoid the heart of the matter. Instead of talking about racism, we deflect our conversation with vague references to "culture," "diversity," "differences," "cross-cultural effectiveness," and so on. Instead of talking about the present-day impact of our history, we congratulate ourselves on how far we have come and how progressive we now seem. Because race has been such a contentious and difficult subject for many, we talk around it rather than address it head-on.

Another failing in many discussions of racism is our desire to emphasize similarities in people and overlook or dismiss the real differences. Many racial dialogues and, in particular, many training programs concentrate solely on the individual, paying little attention to the cultural—the institutional and environmental—influences on the individual. It is often simplistic to ignore or try to transcend the real differences among individuals and between groups of people.

We cannot overlook who and what we are as people. We cannot dismiss the fact that being a woman or a man and being black or white or Asian or Latina or Native American are important aspects of our lives. Our race and gender have an enormous influence on our perspectives and experiences. Moreover, the sociopolitical context in which we live has an even greater impact. We cannot ignore the legacy of racism in

3

our individual and group identities. Each of us must acknowledge and explore these parts of ourselves to discover our unique identities. In fact, Roberts (1975) states that we are not a complete people until we deal with the several significant areas of which we are comprised: personal, sexual, family, ethnic or racial, social class, provincial, and cultural.

Racial identity, in particular, deeply influences how we see the world and interact in it. This concept has long been acknowledged in relation to people of color. Much research has been done on the effects of racism on the self-concept and perspective of people of color. Researchers have only recently begun to explore whiteness, white identity, and the impact on whites of internalized dominance (Kivel, 1995; Hitchcock, 2001). In fact, because whiteness has been considered the norm in the United States, racism has been overlooked as an issue in the white community. The attitude seems to be that if people of color are not physically present, the problem of racism does not exist. Whites easily forget—indeed are seldom aware—that we too are part of a group and are subject to ethnocentrism and a unique collective group experience. In fact, of late, it seems we only want to claim our whiteness when we believe that people of color—in what some term "reverse discrimination"—are discriminating against us. Rarely, however, do we take ownership at the group level for our privilege, power, and perpetuation of racism.

The reality is, racism exists. It has been a part of the American way of life since the first Europeans landed on this continent. Although the United States prides itself on its ideology about human rights and particularly on its philosophy of freedom and equality, the reality is that both historically and currently this country is based on and operates under the doctrine of manifest destiny. We have seen it in the establishment of Native American reservations, in the capture and enslavement of Africans, in the wartime internment of Japanese Americans, in the current, pervasive denial that racism exists, and in the attitude of most white Americans that people of color must "fight" for their rights—the same rights that white Americans enjoy from birth. Racism is manifested not only in the inner cities but equally in the white ghettos of the suburbs, in the South, and in the North. Racism escapes no one. It is a part of us all and has deeply infiltrated the lives and psyches of both the oppressed and the oppressors.

The task that confronts us all is to develop a way of identifying the issues of racism as they exist in the *white* community and helping *white*

4

people to grow and learn about ourselves as whites in this society. How can we help white people to shatter the myths that have sheltered us for so long and to begin focusing on the difficult realities and discrepancies that are present in our society today?

This training program is an attempt to answer that question. It is designed to be used primarily by individuals who are concerned about helping white people to examine our attitudes, behaviors, and the implications of our whiteness in order to become more fully human and to be agents of change. This program has been adapted and used in all sectors of U.S. society—in corporations, in government agencies, in communities, and in educational systems. A major aspect of the program is its flexibility and its ability to be adapted to many different settings.

The program is one of liberation that is designed to go beyond rhetoric by presenting a systematic means of facilitating change in white people's racist attitudes and behaviors. The real test of the program is whether it works. Does it produce change in the attitudes and behaviors of white people? Do we take action? Do we become anti-racist? Research shows that attitudes and behaviors do improve significantly after completion of the workshop. A follow-up study has shown that changes in attitudes and behaviors were maintained. Participants had become actively engaged in developing new curricula for schools, in eliminating racist language, in taking active roles in the governance of their organizations, in examining criteria for hiring, in facilitating workshops on racial awareness, and in educating friends, families, and coworkers. These significant behaviors are evidence that as partners for change white people can effectively address racism in positive, active ways (Katz and Ivey, 1977).

Before turning to the program itself, the facilitator using this handbook should be aware of the premises on which it is based. Chapter 2 offers a theoretical statement and rationale of racism as a white problem, explores the effects of racism on white people, examines the need for change in white people's lives, and looks at various programs that have been developed to confront racism. The need for a systematic, step-by-step training program is established, and some of the implications for research on racism awareness training are examined.

Chapter 3 presents an overview of the training program, together with suggestions on adapting it for different settings, alternative designs, and instructions for the facilitator.

Each stage of the six-stage program is presented in Part II. Specific exercises and experiences are provided to facilitate learning on both the cognitive and the affective level. A list of resources, including reading lists, films, tapes, records, other workshop materials, and suppliers follows the references.

CHAPTER 2

Racism as a White Problem

Over the years attention and concern have been directed to the effect of racism on the quality of life of all Americans. Writers, historians, researchers, and activists have shown that racism is a social, political, economic, and psychological force that has permeated the lives and perspectives of both the oppressed and the oppressors.

More than one hundred years ago W. E. B. Du Bois ([1903] 1994) examined the effects of racism on blacks and whites. More than fifty years ago the Swedish sociologist Gunnar Myrdal (1944) called racism "an American dilemma." Calls for Black, Red, Yellow, and Brown Power echoed in the 1960s. In the decades since, we have seen impassioned debates about affirmative action, busing, integration, "reverse discrimination," racial profiling, Confederate flag support, apologies for slavery, reparations, ebonics, and a host of other racial issues.

In 1997 President Clinton convened the President's Initiative on Race. The commission spent a year investigating the current state of race relations in the United States, talking to people around the country, engaging in a national dialogue, researching statistics, and so forth. In its 1998 report, the commission wrote:

> Our Nation still struggles with the impact of its past policies, practices, and attitudes based on racial difference. Race and ethnicity will have profound impacts on the extent to which a person is fully included in American society and provided the equal opportunity and equal protection promised to all Americans. All of these characteristics continue to affect an individual's opportunity to receive an education, acquire the skills necessary to maintain a good job, have access to adequate health care, and receive equal justice under the law. (2)

This is a cogent analysis, but like so much of what has been written and said about race relations in America, it focuses almost exclusively on the problems racism creates for people of color. This is a critical component of any examination of racism, of course, but it turns the focus away from the cause of the problem to its effects. And it leaves unexplored the impact of racism on white people.

It is essential to focus on racism as it affects the oppressors or dominant group. This chapter seeks to establish the nature of racism as a white problem, describe its effects on whites both psychologically and intellectually, and discuss the processes that are necessary to bring about change in the attitudes and behaviors of whites.

There is a growing tendency to address this aspect of racism, but few strategies or materials have been designed to raise the consciousness of white people, to help us identify racism in ourselves and others, or to develop skills to facilitate change in the white community. Although there is a great deal of rhetoric about the need for change and the destructiveness of racism, the strategies developed to alleviate the problem often are merely new programs aimed at people of color. The victim, not the victimizer, once again becomes the target for change. The symptoms are attacked instead of the cause. For example, even in multicultural education programs that are attempting to break down rigid cultural barriers, we find a great deal of emphasis on appreciation of differences but little implementation of these concepts in all-white areas, where the cultural isolation may be the greatest. Until the real perpetuators of racism are confronted and educated, little will change. Until the discrepancies between our nation's ideals and the reality are uncovered, white Americans will continue to live a personal lie and maintain a false sense of identity in the world.

Racism as a White Problem

To examine racism in America today, one must first explore its roots and development. White racism has a history spanning more than four hundred years (Bennett, 1966; Jordan, 1968; Kovel, 1970). The foundations of racism and the present-day racist system were established in western European, especially English, ideology and language. According to Schwartz and Disch (1970:6), "By the time the first English colonists had arrived in the New World they had already inherited a host of associations tied to the word 'black' which became important as men put language to use in first defining and later justifying the status they desired of non-whites."

When the colonists arrived on this continent, these negative attitudes of whites toward peoples of color were codified in racist practices and policies (Lacy, 1972). This is evident in the account by Joyce (n.d.):

8

From the time the first Native American "Indian" died at the hands of a European settler (if not before), the United States has held white supremacy as a dominant theme in its institutional and cultural life. The "New World" civilizations ultimately destroyed nearly one-half of the "Indian" population (genocide by any criteria), defined in its basic political document the black person as three-fifths of a man, and created a chattel slavery system more dehumanizing and destructive than any the world has even known. (1)

Such is the basis of racism in the United States. From the time of formalized slavery to the present, whites have oppressed people of color through the perpetuation of racism at every level of life. It is present in our institutions, our culture, and our individual actions. Despite all the history books, White people often are not knowledgeable about the tradition of racism in the United States and the way in which the past informs the present. The President's Initiative on Race (1998) determined that

[t]he absence of both knowledge and understanding about the role race has played in our collective history continues to make it difficult to find solutions that will improve race relations, eliminate disparities, and create equal opportunities in all areas of American life. This absence also contributes to conflicting views on race and racial progress held by Americans of color and white Americans. (3)

This is similar to the Kerner Commission findings thirty years earlier. Young (1970) supported the Kerner Commission's findings:

Most Americans get awfully uptight about the charge of racism, since most people are not conscious of what racism really is. Racism is not a desire to wake up every morning and lynch a black man from a tall tree. It is not engaging in vulgar epithets. These kinds of people are just fools. It is the day-to-day indignities, the subtle humiliations that are so devastating. Racism is the assumptions of superiority of one group over another, with all the gross arrogance that goes along with it. Racism is a part of us. The Kerner Commission has said that if you have been an observer you have been racist; if you have stood by idly, you are racist. (730)

If racism is not defined strictly by overt actions, then how is it created and perpetuated?

What underlies so much of racism in the United States—especially racism that is not perpetuated by traditional "white supremacist" groups but by our institutions and by well-meaning white people—is the concept of white privilege. White privilege is often invisible to those who possess it. We attribute our success and opportunities to our own hard work, moral character, and overall worthiness. We do not recognize the degree to which racial status and an uneven playing field gives us an advantage.

Jensen (1998) characterized white privilege by identifying its influence in his own life:

> All through my life, I have soaked up benefits for being white. I grew up in fertile farm country taken by force from non-white indigenous people. I was educated in a well-funded, virtually all-white public school system in which I learned that white people like me made this country great. There I also was taught a variety of skills, including how to take standardized tests written by and for white people. All my life I have been hired for jobs by white people. I was accepted for graduate school by white people. And I was hired for a teaching position at the predominantly white University of Texas, which had a white president, in a college headed by a white dean and in a department with a white chairman that at the time had one non-white tenured professor.
>
> There certainly is individual variation in experience. Some white people have had it easier than me, probably because they came from wealthy families that gave them even more privilege. Some white people have had it tougher than me because they came from poorer families. White women face discrimination I will never know. But, in the end, white people all have drawn on white privilege somewhere in their lives. (C-1)

Even today, in an age of diversity initiatives and affirmative action and changing demographics, this experience is not uncommon. It points out that white people enjoy the spoils of racism, even if we do not believe we are acting in racist ways, a fact too often missed by many of us. Whether or not we exhibit racism in our individual acts and behaviors, we willingly participate in institutions and systems built on racist foundations, as described by Dixon (2000):

The white club does not require that all members be strong advocates of white supremacy, merely that they defer to the prejudices of others.

So racial oppression is not the work of racists. It is maintained by the principal institutions of society, including the schools (which define "excellence"), the labor market (which defines "employment"), the legal system (which defines "crime"), the welfare system (which defines "poverty"), the medical industry (which defines "health"), and the family (which defines "kinship"). Many of these institutions are administered by people who would be offended if accused of complicity with racial oppression.

McIntosh (1988) found the connection between whiteness and oppression when she began to list some of the advantages white people experience in U.S. society and realized that they go beyond mere "privilege": "We usually think of privilege as being a favored state, whether earned or conferred by birth or luck. Yet some of the conditions [in the United States] work to systematically overempower certain groups. Such privilege simply *confers dominance* because of one's race" (3). Racism is a white problem in that its development and perpetuation rest with white people. Whites created racism through the establishment of policies and practices that serve to benefit us and continue to oppress people of color. It is perpetuated by whites through our conscious or unconscious support of a culture and institutions that are founded on racist policies and practices.

Effects of Racism on White People

Privilege is probably the most obvious effect of racism for white people. In fact, the very term "white race" is a definition of status, not genetics. As scientists have noted, race is a social construct, not a biological one. There are other implications for whites too.

One is what the Harvard psychologist Maureen Walker has termed "internalized dominance"—the inbred assumption among whites that superiority over people of color is our birthright. This attitude infects all interactions with people of color and influences our immediate reactions to their competence, talents, and achievements. It poses a great barrier for whites by preventing us from engaging fully with people of color and by supporting a deluded view of the world and our place in it (Larkin and Walker, 1994).

The idea that racism hurts whites has not been fully explored, but it is not new. Du Bois (1920) recognized it nearly a century ago, in noting that he somehow felt sorry for whites and our warped sense of superiority:

> But where is the misfortune? Mine? Am I, in my blackness, the sole sufferer? I suffer. And yet, somehow, above the suffering, above the shackled anger that beats the bars, above the hurt that crazes there surges in me a vast pity—pity for a people imprisoned and enthralled, hampered and made miserable for such a cause, for such a phantasy! (33–34)

It has been hypothesized that in a somewhat different way racism is just as dehumanizing for whites as it is for people of color (Du Bois ([1903] 1994); Kovel, 1970; Cobbs, 1972). Berry pointed this out in *The Hidden Wound* (1970):

> If white people have suffered less obviously from racism than black people, they have nevertheless suffered greatly; the cost has been greater perhaps than we yet know. If the white [people have] inflicted the wound of racism upon black [people], the cost has been that [they] would receive the mirror image of that wound into [themselves]. (2)

But what is the nature of this wound? In what ways are white people harmed?

One way is our limited set of competencies for living in a diverse and multicultural world. Ironically, the "white perspective" that has so long been a socioeconomic boon and that has disadvantaged people of color has become an impediment. My work as an organizational consultant and change agent over the past thirty years has put me in touch with dozens of companies and corporations that have become convinced that a monocultural environment that values sameness limits their success (Katz and Miller, 1995). The movement in business toward leveraging diversity and creating a more inclusive work culture is not primarily a reaction to legal and social pressures; it is a bottom-line productivity initiative predicated on the notion that differences in experiences, points of view, skills, styles, interests, and so forth, are enriching and valuable. And to create such a culture means that the normative white culture on which most organizations have been built must change.

Among the many examples I could cite is the case of an engineering firm whose primary clients were located in major metropolitan areas. They had hired a number of new engineers, all from the same mid-western college. All were young white men with very high GPAs. Most of them were failing at the company. Their work involved partnering with a diverse population of clients, and their very limited experiences placed them at a severe disadvantage. They had trouble communicating effectively, sharing ideas, and working across differences.

In general, this is a competence missing in many white people: the ability to step outside of our own experience—which we have so long perceived as the *one right way*—and work effectively with others across racial differences. As the business world becomes increasingly global and diverse, this is becoming a major deficiency, especially for those who aspire to leadership positions. But even outside the corporate culture, the need to partner across differences is a major component of contemporary life.

In addition, there has been increased discussion about the psychological toll of racism on white people. Racism has been diagnosed as a form of schizophrenia in that there is a large gap between what whites believe and what we actually practice, which causes us to live in a state of psychological stress (Allen, 1971; Bidol, 1971). Myrdal (1944), in his study of the "race problem" in America, concluded that racism underlies every facet of life in the United States—political, economic, and social. At the bottom of the problem, however, he found the white citizens' moral dilemma:

> the deep cultural and psychological conflict among the American people of American ideals of equality, freedom, God-given dignity of the individual, inalienable rights on the one hand, against practices of discrimination, humiliation, insult, denial of opportunity to Negroes and others in a racist society on the other. (xxi)

Myrdal was telling us that at the heart of racism in the United States is a discrepancy between attitude and action, between thought and deed. The white American citizen talks about equality and says that she or he believes in it. Yet alongside this profession is the truth of oppression and denial of selfhood to citizens of other colors (Katz and Ivey, 1977). (In reality, a paradox exists: the United States *is* a land of opportunity, and clearly we have made progress with respect to what individuals and groups can achieve, but the United States is also a land of oppression, in whose systems and structures discrimination, prejudice, and racism are still embedded.)

Other authors offer theories that see racism as a disease. Thomas and Sillen (1972) find that racism is deeply rooted in personality. Comer (1991), a psychiatrist, elaborates on this point in his analysis of racism. He describes it as a "low level defense and adjustment mechanism similar to the manner in which individuals utilize psyche defenses and adjustment mechanisms to deal with anxiety" (311). Delaney (1990) identifies the disease by breaking down racism into elements that include acting out, denial of reality, projection, transference of blame, disassociation, and justification. All these elements are basic characteristics of destructive behavior. The psychologist Kenneth Clark (1963) noted that in "normal forms of expressions of prejudice among average Americans, one observes certain types of reactions which, if demonstrated with other members of an individual's own race, would be considered symptoms of emotional disturbance" (77). All these analyses clearly indicate that racism is a pervasive form of mental illness.

It is crucial to explore how the disease is manifested in observable traits and ideologies. One way is through the delusion of white superiority (Jordan, 1968; Citron, 1969; Kovel, 1970; Welsing, 1970; Bidol, 1971; Brown, 1972). Racism and ethnocentric ideologies envelop white people so that we are unable to experience ourselves and our culture *as it is*. Du Bois, in his essay "The Souls of White Folk" (1920), looked at how the attitude of superiority is displayed in whites. Du Bois saw it as arrogance coupled with a disdain for everyone and everything nonwhite. This has been perpetuated through omission and emphasis, leading to a belief that everything great that was ever done in the world was the work of whites.

The belief that "white is right" often leaves whites confused about our identity (Bidol, 1971). Beck (1973) stated, "The confusion of the meaning of whiteness leads many whites to think that all America is white" (23). Because U.S. culture is centered on white norms, white people rarely have to come to terms with that part of our identity. Ask a white person her or his race and you may get the response "Italian," "Jewish," "Irish," "English," and so on. *White people do not see ourselves as white.* This is a way of denying responsibility for perpetuating the racist system and being part of the problem. Not identifying as white—separating oneself from white culture—allows one to disown one's racism. Lack of understanding of self owing to a poor sense of identity causes whites to develop a negative attitude toward people of color on both

14

a conscious and a subconscious level (Quarles, 1964; Schwartz and Disch, 1970; Allen, 1971).

Whites who are conscientious about race and eager to help dismantle racism often feel guilty about our privilege and the unintentional ways we have wielded our power to the detriment of people of color. In his essay "White Privilege Shapes the U.S." (1998), Jensen rejects this psychological trap:

> I don't feel guilty. Guilt is appropriate when one has wronged another, when one has something to feel guilty about. In my life I have felt guilty for racist or sexist things I have said or done, even when they were done unconsciously. But that is guilt I felt because of specific acts, not for the color of my skin. Also, focusing on individual guilt feelings is counterproductive when it leads us to ponder the issue from a psychological point of view instead of a moral and political one. So, I cannot, and indeed should not, feel either guilty or proud about being white, because it is a state of being I have no control over. (C-1)

He is careful not to use this as a rationalization or an excuse for inaction:

> I don't feel guilty about being white in a white supremacist society, but I feel an especially strong moral obligation to engage in collective political activity to try to change the society because I benefit from the injustice. I try to be reflective and accountable, though I am human and I make mistakes. I think a lot about how I may be expressing racism unconsciously, but I don't lay awake at night feeling guilty. Guilt is not a particularly productive emotion, and I don't wallow in it. (C-1)

Some of the literature on racism focuses on the development of racist attitudes in children. Goodman's study (1964) showed that children are infected with racism as early as age four. She elicited concepts and feelings on race from white four-year-olds and concluded from their remarks and their tone that by that age they had already internalized feelings of superiority. Singh and Yancey (1974) found negative racial attitudes among white first-graders. Morland (1962) noted that the preference for being white and the negative attitude of white children toward blacks were based not necessarily on direct negative contact with blacks but on subtle communication from parents, teachers, the media, and others. Other studies have found a strong preference among very young white children for the color white and a negative connotation for the color black. This negative connotation is transferred from the color black to black people (Greenwald and Oppenheim, 1968; Robinson and Spaights, 1969; Singh and Yancey, 1974; Kivel, 1995).

In a landmark experiment, an elementary school teacher divided her students into two groups based on blue or brown eye color. One group was given preferential treatment while the other experienced undeniable prejudice based on a natural trait over which they had no control. On the first day the blue eyes experienced being "one up." On the second day, they reversed roles. Not only did the disadvantaged group experience firsthand what discrimination felt like, the experiment showed the privileged group falling into oppressive behaviors and quickly adapting to their role as oppressors. The teacher talked about how sobering it was to witness the group that was in the "one-up" position and how easily they took active measures to keep the other group in its place (Peters, 1970).

In *Learning to Be White* (1999), Thandeka interviewed hundreds of white people and asked them to recount the first time they realized they were white. Many told stories of early childhood: a five-year-old American girl living in Mexico was told not to play with the local children; a five-year-old boy sensed his family's discomfort when he invited black neighbors to his birthday party; a four-year-old boy's parents drove him through the black section of town so that he would not stare at black people during an upcoming trip to New York City. That her subjects remember these experiences much later in life indicates the impression they make on young minds and how early reinforcement of racist attitudes begins.

Citron (1969) best sums up the overall effects of racism on the white child:

> White-centeredness is not the reality of his [*sic*] world, but he is under the illusion that it is. It is thus impossible for him to deal accurately or adequately with the universe of human and social relationships. . . . He also learns salience, that is, what portions of his environment are important to him, and to which he must react. He learns in his white world the importance of reacting in a certain way to skin color. . . . Children who develop this pattern

16

learn dependence on a psychological and moral crutch which inhibits and deforms the growth of a healthy and responsible personality. . . . Children who develop in this way are robbed of opportunities for emotional and intellectual growth, stunted in basic development of the self so that they cannot experience or accept humanity. This is a personality outcome in which it is quite possible to build into a child a great feeling and compassion for animals and an unconscious fear and rejection of differing human beings. Such persons are by no means prepared to live and move with either appreciation or effectiveness in today's world. (14–16)

It becomes sadly evident from these studies that the psychological disorder of racism is deeply embedded in white people from a very early age on both a conscious and an unconscious level.

Racism has also been found to cripple white people intellectually (Citron, 1969; Beck, 1973; Daniels, 1974). In their study of institutional racism in America, Knowles and Prewitt (1969) found that white children are miseducated. U.S. history courses and foreign affairs are distorted through superficial and inconsistent treatment of people of color and their contributions to the world. Racial issues are rarely dealt with realistically or recorded accurately. Overall, texts and information reemphasize white Americans and omit other Americans' contributions to society. White people, as well as people of color, have been miseducated about our historical roots (Daniels, 1973).

Citron (1969) summarizes the effects of racism on whites:

The white ghetto creates exactly the kinds of beings who act as if they are on the other side of a thick pane of glass, not only from Negroes, but from the real world. They are blandly unconcerned, unaware, operating in an aura of assumed rightness and unconscious superiority.

The white-centered, provincial, insulated, imperialistic mentality of white ghettoization acts as blinders over the eyes of children, and cotton in their ears, imprisoning the minds, shackling the spirits, crippling the personality. (12)

In summary, it is clear that racism has severely hindered white people's psychological and intellectual development. In psychological terms racism has deluded whites into a false sense of superiority that

17

has left us in a pathological and schizophrenic state. In intellectual terms racism has resulted in miseducation about history, the contributions of people of color, and the role of white people in present-day culture. The intellectual perspective and growth potential of whites has been severely limited by racism.

Mechanisms for Change

What can be done to address these situations? One important step is to get whites and the white community to recognize racism as a white problem and then accept responsibility for dismantling it.

Malcolm X clearly endorsed the idea that whites must take action among ourselves if we want to make an impact on racism: "Whites who are sincere should organize themselves and figure out some strategies to break down the prejudice that exists in white communities. This is where they can function more intelligently and more effectively, in the white community itself, and this has never been done" (Breitman, 1970, 164). Carmichael (Carmichael and Hamilton, 1967) put it more bluntly: "If the white man wants to help he can go home and free his own people."

Several steps are necessary to achieve this "freedom" and self-awareness. One is the recognition that white culture and white privilege exist. They are not theoretical concepts but tangible, visible aspects of life in the United States.

Another major challenge is initiating conversation about race among whites. Many white people in the United States are uncomfortable discussing racism as a problem that still exists. As Hitchcock has noted (2002): "[White people] love to talk about our good intentions, the progress we've made, and how we aspire to equality. But if the conversation suggests that we may have some more work to do on these issues, some people head for the door" (5).

The need for reeducation of white people is stressed in a statement by the United States Commission on Civil Rights (1970): "The principal task of those white Americans combating racism lies with the white community, rather than within the non-white communities" (39). The President's Initiative on Race (1998) identified "Ten Things Every American Should Do to Promote Racial Reconciliation," many of them aimed specifically at the white community:

1. Make a commitment to become informed about people from other races and cultures.

2. If it is not your inclination to think about race, commit at least 1 day each month to thinking about how issues of racial prejudice and privilege might be affecting each person you come in contact with that day.
3. In your life, make a conscious effort to get to know people of other races.
4. Make a point to raise your concerns about comments or actions that appear prejudicial, even if you are not the targets of these actions.
5. Initiate a constructive dialogue on race within your workplace, school, neighborhood, or religious community.
6. Support institutions that promote racial inclusion.
7. Participate in a community project to reduce racial disparities in opportunity and well-being.
8. Insist that institutions that teach us about our community accurately reflect the diversity of our Nation.
9. Visit other areas of the city, region, or country that allow you to experience parts of other cultures, beyond their food.
10. Advocate that groups you can influence (whether you work as a volunteer or employee) examine how they can increase their commitment to reducing racial disparities, lessening discrimination, and improving race relations. (102–4)

These are individual actions that can lay the groundwork for changing one's attitudes and actions. To move beyond that into education and the kind of community-wide change that undermines systematic racism, large-group methods are required.

One mechanism designed to lessen racial and ethnic tensions is the interracial encounter group (Cobbs, 1972; Kranz, 1972; Walker and Hamilton, 1973; Wilkinson, 1973). This process grew out of sensitivity training techniques (Marrow, 1967) and developed into a more structured, confrontational group (Winter, 1971). The technique deals with the participants' affective level of consciousness. The basic premise of the encounter group process is that interracial communications will improve and subsequently lead to positive action (Walker and Hamilton, 1973).

Rubin's work with T-groups indicated that they lessen racial prejudice. At the end of a T-group made up of eight whites and two blacks, Rubin (1967) found a significant decrease in racial prejudice. The encounter group of Walker and Hamilton (1973), consisting of six blacks, four Chicanos, and four whites, also appeared to result in a reduction of interracial tensions. A similar model was developed to increase teachers' capacity to relate to others regardless of race (Goldin, 1970). Still another interracial confrontation group, this one in a junior college, produced some positive results: both black and white participants felt better about one other (Kranz, 1972). The video *The Color of Fear* (Wah 1994), in which a diverse group of men conduct a candid and often heated discussion about racism, has been highly instructive to white audiences and provides a stark view of the reality people of color face every day.

Although it appears that the interracial encounter group is a useful tool for changing attitudes, one must look deeper at the data presented. One problem that arises with interracial group experiences is that the functioning of the groups may itself contribute to supporting racism. Kranz (1972), in his description of his racial confrontation group, opens by saying:

> Historically, whites have exhorted non-whites to make changes so that they would be acceptable as full-fledged Americans. However, events in the U.S. have shown the dishonesty and tragedy of this emphasis. Therefore, a major focus of each group was to help whites see that they must learn and change within themselves if further violence is to be avoided. (70)

Ironically, the same condition may exist in similar interracial group processes; that is, the responsibility to facilitate change remains focused on the historically oppressed group. People of color often feel they are placed in the position of teaching white people, the same responsibility that Kranz notes they have historically been given. This is a dynamic to be careful of when working in interracial groups. The overall tone for the group must be one of sharing and learning together, instead of one group bearing the burden of educating the other.

Obviously, there are many approaches to change, and clearly, given the power and history of racism in the United States, no one mechanism is the cure-all. That many school systems are creating a more multicultural curriculum begins to address the miseducation that has plagued us for too long. However, too many curricula maintain a primarily white perspective on history and then celebrate other cultures with "Black History Month," "Hispanic History Month," and so on, to discuss the contributions of people of color. This recognition represents progress but often relegates these historical achievements to the same second-class status that people of color themselves have received.

Many universities are developing departments, curricula, and experiences that address the issues of racism and attempt to bridge the racial gap. However, these ways of addressing racism are usually not woven in to the culture, structure, and institutional operations of the universities. Most of these attempts focus on a cognitive approach to change; the assumption is that if people have more knowledge they will, in fact, change. For some, this may be true. There is very little data on the success of these mechanisms in changing racist attitudes and behaviors, however. Still, given the nature of the miseducation, the cognitive approach appears to be greatly needed. Malcolm X supported this position:

> If the entire American population were properly educated—by properly educated, I mean given the true picture of the history and contributions of the black man—I think many whites would be less racist in their feelings. They would have more respect for the black man as a human being. Knowing what the black man's contributions to science and civilization have been in the past, the white man's feelings of superiority would be at least partially negated. . . . So it takes education to eliminate it. And just because you have colleges and universities doesn't mean you have education. The colleges and universities in the American educational system are skillfully used to miseducate. (Breitman, 1970, 160–61)

Although these efforts appear to be important in changing white people's racist attitudes and behavior, they fall short in that they do not deal with the psychological and affective sides of those attitudes.

A significant approach to combating racism that has emerged in the past two decades is the development of multicultural curricula for school classrooms. Teachers today at almost every educational level and in nearly every area of the country have access to a broad spectrum of instructional materials that give students a diverse view of humankind and a more accurate understanding of the contributions of people of color. (Not all school systems take advantage of this, of course.) Unfortunately, these programs rarely focus on white culture as a phenomenon in itself. It is assumed that only white history is being taught in the schools and that therefore there is no need to give it additional attention.

21

Although this assumption is partly correct, in that white history has been taught as "American" history, the effect on children—both white and of color—is to perpetuate an erroneous view of being white. What is needed is reeducation and a realistic focus on the role that white people and white culture have played in shaping U.S. history. This crucial step is often overlooked.

Finally, in multicultural education programs there is much discussion of the need for students of color to develop a positive sense of identity—the assumption being that whites already have that positive sense of self. But whites also need to identify ourselves as white and feel good about it. This does not minimize the need of those who have been oppressed but rather acknowledges faulty assumptions and generalizations that have been made about whites for too long.

While it is important to acknowledge racism and its detrimental effects and to make explicit the negative dimensions of white culture, it is also important that being white is seen as a positive attribute. Pinderhughes (1989) made this point when discussing the futility of guilt and shame:

> Few whites are honestly able to say that being white is an identity that brings them a sense of pride. Although some may feel that being white means being powerful, lucky, comfortable, and secure, it also can mean confusion, entrapment, and threatened self-esteem, hardly attributes that would promote helpfulness to people-of- colour, who may be dealing with such consequences themselves. Changing the meaning of white to a more positive one thus becomes an important step in preparation for white effectiveness in changing the oppressed condition. (3)

There is a growing body of research that looks at white identity development and its evolution. Earlier research on black identity development (Cross, 1971; Thomas, 1971; Jackson, 1976) has led to the identification of its white counterpart (Helms, 1993; Hardiman, 1994). Being an "unconscious white person" is only one stage in this development; in other stages, whites learn to develop a positive sense of being white, without absolving ourselves of the responsibilities we bear for racism and other *isms*. White identity development explores the stages of growth through which whites progress as we come to grips with the understanding of racism, own our racial identity, and find a way to take positive action with a positive sense of self.

22

One technique designed to address the issue of being white is the white-on-white training group. Expanding on the belief that white people must work within the white community (Cleaver, 1968; Terry, 1970; Steinberg, n.d.), these groups were developed so that whites could explore racism without exploiting people of color (Bidol, 1971; Moore, 1973; Edler, 1974). Some of the white-on-white experiences focus on affective issues (Moore, 1973), while others are structured to deal with cognitive issues (Bidol, 1971; Timmel, n.d.). The purpose of these groups is to create a positive change in attitudes and behavior so that white people take action to combat racism (Terry, 1970).

Moore (1973) has shown that this technique is successful. He facilitated a number of white-on-white workshops and found a positive change in white teachers' racial attitudes. In this area there is a great need for further development of resources, specifically, a developmental process to assure positive change in both attitudes and behaviors.

It is not easy to create opportunities for whites to come together to talk about whiteness and understand our roles and privilege with respect to racism. Many of our models for white-only groups are racist supremacy groups. When I recently held a seminar entitled "What White People Can Do About Racism" at a Baltimore hotel, the staff was skittish about putting a sign in the lobby. They feared that guests and employees would think we were a white supremacist group. Jeff Hitchcock, who founded and heads the Center for the Study of White American Culture, a multiracial group committed to addressing white racism, constantly encounters misperceptions of his group's intent.

White-on-white groups, though, are an essential element for creating an environment in which white people can explore our racism and our identity and share our experiences as a foundation for action. Such sessions work in concert with efforts to bring a diverse group of people together to address racism as partners and allies for change. Whites need this to achieve the self-examination and to do the hard work of dismantling racism. This book grew out of that need.

CHAPTER 3

How to Use This Program

This chapter provides the facilitator with an overview of the white-on-white systematic training program.

Objectives and Goals

The overall objectives of this program are to help white people become aware of how racism affects our lives, our institutions, our perspectives, and our actions and to help change our assumptions and behaviors. The program strives to help whites understand that racism in the United States is a systemic and institutional problem, one that whites as a group are responsible for, and that being white implies being racist. This does not mean that people of color do not have any work to do with respect to dealing with and addressing racism. Through white awareness, however, the focus is whites—our responsibility, our privilege, and our need to take action.

This understanding is achieved most successfully through (1) confrontation—identifying the discrepancies that exist between what one says and what one does; and (2) reeducation—examining history and perspectives through new perceptual filters. If participants can recognize the inconsistencies between ideologies and behaviors at the institutional and cultural levels, they can better understand how their own attitudes and behaviors have been permeated by racism. Once whites become aware of this dimension, we can more easily own our racism at the individual level and develop ways to confront it.

Unlike many racism awareness programs, this one is not designed to produce guilt or to confront people in a way that puts them down. Guilt often serves to entrench attitudes—to keep people feeling sorry for themselves or others. This program is designed to help white people become free of the perspectives that have trapped us in our views of ourselves and in our interactions with other whites and with people of color.

Once participants have developed an awareness of the problem of racism on the institutional, cultural, and individual levels, it is crucial that their behavior change in line with that awareness. One helpful way to produce that change has been used by Uhlemann (1968) with encounter groups. The participants developed an objective before a marathon group experience. The objective was to identify a specific behavioral change. I have also used this approach successfully in this program. All too often whites, when faced with the reality of racism, can feel overwhelmed and believe that the problem is insurmountable. By identifying one behavior change, one action we can take, the fear of making additional changes was lessened. Participants could then recognize the choices they could make with regard to their own behavior and begin to address racism on a personal as well as an institutional level.

This program consists of six stages of development and appropriate exercises to work through each stage. If the goals of this program are reached, by the end of the workshop the participants will be able to

1) name and clearly define and differentiate the concepts of bias, bigotry, prejudice, and racism;
2) describe and examine racism in its institutional, cultural, and individual forms;
3) identify and articulate personal feelings and fears about the issue of racism;
4) define ways in which one's own attitudes and behaviors are representative of racism in the United States; and
5) develop and act on specific strategies designed to challenge racism on an institutional and individual level.

Assumptions

The following assumptions form the basis of this training program.

Racism is a predominantly white problem. White people are responsible for the perpetuation of white racism in a white racist system. Our submersion in this system makes it difficult for us to realize the extent to which we perpetuate and support racism in a multitude of ways every day.

All Americans have feelings and thoughts about the issue of racism. Virtually no person of any racial group in the United States can grow up without being exposed to and developing some prejudiced attitudes about another person or group. Whites, being part of a white racist system, have many unresolved thoughts, feelings, and questions centering on the dynamics and issues of racism. Socially and psychologically,

25

racism prevents whites from escaping from ethnocentrism. In the white world, whites subconsciously learn to fear and reject persons who are different (Citron, 1969). Such emotions affect our relationships with each other, our own mental health, and our interactions with people of other racial groups.

White people can learn about racism with other white people. Racist attitudes are often developed without any personal exposure to people of color. Whites, therefore, can begin the process of learning about racism with other whites who have begun to explore their own racism. This approach avoids exploiting people of color as white people's educators.

Whites need to be reeducated. We have grown up in a system that has ingrained in us racist ideologies and attitudes. We need to be in a trusting and safe environment in which we can strip away some of these old ideologies and perceptions and become open to the realities of racism cognitively and emotionally. This will enable us to understand ourselves better as white people, as well as to explore our role in combating racism in American society.

It is physically, socially, and psychologically advantageous for whites to learn about racism for our own survival. Whites make up only one-tenth of the world's population; people of color constitute the other nine-tenths. Even in the United States, white people comprise a steadily shrinking percentage of the population and in some cities no longer represent the majority. Many businesses have taken up the call for greater diversity and the development of a new skill set to respond effectively to an increasingly diverse marketplace.

For our own survival, both physical and economic, whites must change our racist system and attitudes so that we can live and work effectively together. We must learn new skills to partner, interact, and collaborate across racial lines. We must move beyond tolerating differences to seeking out and valuing such differences. We must move from fear and avoidance to action and engagement (Miller and Katz, 2002). The potential of creating truly inclusive and nonexploitive organizations and society exists only if whites are willing to take vigilant action to address racism in all its manifestations. This entails a whole new perspective, a new set of assumptions, and new actions and ways of being. Organizations are beginning to see the business imperative for having a more diverse workforce. It has become not only a moral imperative but a survival issue as well. If we, as whites, intend to remain competitive, to be able to live our lives as full human beings, it is in our best interest to learn about and deal with racism.

This program is a step in a process and not an end in itself. The women's movement taught us that it is not only important for men to do their work with respect to sexism, it is also essential for women and men to explore perspectives in a supportive environment. Men are better able to improve relationships with the other gender once they understand their role in perpetuating sexism, the institutional manifestations of sexism, and the individual actions needed for change. Similarly, women need to do our own work—to address our internalized oppression, to recognize how sexism in our institutions and culture has affected us, and to bring that understanding and awareness to everything we do. It is also crucial for women and men to come together to develop new organizational models that are not gender based and new ways to partner effectively across differences. This process is also true for people of color and whites.

If whites are in a setting in which we can develop our consciousness of our whiteness and our racism, we can then move toward developing relationships with other whites and with people of color that are more authentic and less oppressive. This training program is a step in that direction. Clearly, one training program cannot alleviate all of one's internalized dominance or racism. It serves as one dimension of this process.

Out of these assumptions, this program was developed and designed to help whites become more aware of racism and to provide mechanisms by which we can move in a more positive and healthier direction. To use this program effectively, the facilitator should keep in mind several key factors. Above all, you should have a good understanding of racism. This includes both awareness on a personal level of your own prejudices and assumption and a deep understanding and ability to analyze and describe racism on an institutional and cultural level. To facilitate this program—or any program dealing with racism—without a good understanding and working knowledge of the sociohistorical context and dynamics of racism not only will cause the program to be ineffective but also will perpetuate the participants' racism, as well as your own.

You should be open to your own learning needs and you should be a role model whose ideas, attitudes, and values can be tested by individuals and the group. Your willingness to disclose your own struggles with racism and the areas that are still unresolved for you will be most helpful in the learning process of others. The facilitator who is a role model will help participants in their own self-examination. It is

27

important to remember that racism runs deep and that we can never be completely cured of its effects. What we can do is constantly learn, grow, and be conscious of racism in us and around us.

The facilitator should also have solid group-process skills. A climate of trust must be established so that participants feel safe exploring their attitudes and behaviors and comfortable disclosing them to others in the group. It is essential for the facilitator to recognize how difficult it is for most white people to come to grips with racism. For many whites, facing this part of who we are elicits anger and shame. Therefore, demonstrating support and concern for the individuals in this experience is crucial. While dealing with the content issues—for example, defining racism or exploring institutional racism—the facilitator must also be aware of the process issues: how people are feeling (defensive, fearful, closed, guilty, etc.), how they respond to one another, and so on. Both the content and the process are necessary for effective education. It will be useful to read through the entire program before using it, so that you can get a clear picture of both the content and the process issues that may emerge.

It is essential to remember that this program is a beginning, not an end. It is designed to give participants an in-depth view of racism and to move them toward action based on their understanding of white racism developed with the support of other white people. From there the participants can continue to explore each form of racism and become actively involved in developing ways to address it. As a result of this experience, white people come to accept being white. This provides a foundation from which to develop relationships with both whites and members of other races that are nonexploitive and nonoppressive. For many whites, this process moves us from a place of fear to a place of more authentic engagement and interaction. This training program thus represents a first step in uncovering the deeply rooted disease of racism and a first step in the direction of liberation for all people.

Format

The six stages of the training program are presented in Part II of this book. Each stage appears in the following format: (1) an introduction, followed by sections on rationale and method, and (2) the exercises themselves. A list of exercises faces the opening page of each stage. Materials used in the exercises (questionnaires, forms, etc.) follow the discussion of the exercise.

28

Stage 1 lays the groundwork for participants to understand racism in society and in ourselves. In this first stage, the key concepts of prejudice and racism are explored. The participants become aware that *power* is the major factor that distinguishes racism from prejudice.

Stage 2 probes institutional racism. Participants are confronted with the discrepancies in U.S. ideology and behavior.

Stage 3 is designed to help participants sort through the feelings and reactions that were triggered in the previous stages. Feelings of fear, projection, shame, and guilt are brought to the surface.

Stage 4 explores cultural racism, including an examination of language, music, norms, and values. Attention is focused on white ethnocentrism and cultural differences.

Stage 5 focuses on the meaning of whiteness and helps participants to claim their white identity as an essential part of themselves. In this stage, participants explore their own prejudices and roles in supporting racism. Stage 5 helps participants to develop a more positive racial identity.

Stage 6 helps participants to develop specific action strategies to combat personal and institutional racism and define their next steps in becoming anti-racist.

A list of recommended books, articles, Web sites, study guides, videos, and workshops that are useful to the learning process follows the references.

Groups: Why All White?

This program is designed for all-white groups so that the participants can

1) establish a climate that focuses on the meaning of being white and on developing a sense of whiteness as part of one's identity;
2) explore racist attitudes and behaviors in a climate of trust and support; and
3) accomplish this learning without relying on people of color as the "teachers" and without merely reacting to or denying their life experiences.

Facilitators

This program can be staffed in a number of ways. It can be facilitated by one person or by co-trainers. The staff must have a deep understanding of the issues of racism. It is useful to have a woman-man team and to draw analogies to other forms of oppression (e.g., sexism, ageism, heterosexism, anti-Semitism) where possible. The program can be cofacilitated by an interracial team, though there is the risk that participants will assume that the person of color speaks for all individuals of that identity group or that the group will constantly be asking the leader of color about her or his experiences with racism. The interracial team is useful if both facilitators can take advantage of these dynamics to enhance learning. It is essential to keep a watchful eye on that part of the process.

Designs: Application to Your Setting

This program can be used and applied in many contexts and formats, depending on the setting and time limitations. The key to an effective program is to maintain flexibility and adaptability. Imagination and knowledge of the group's needs are vital. The more the content of the program focuses on issues that reflect the participants' world, the greater the investment they are likely to make and the greater the degree of learning. Whether you are working with managers in the corporate sector, educators, counselors, administrators, students, religious groups, community agencies, or government officials, the program is easily adaptable.

Given the focus on racism and the systematic nature of the program, many of the experiences can be used in any setting. It will be most important to use your participants' contexts in Stage 2. For example, in Exercise 8, "Mini-Lecture: Kinds and Levels of Racism," you should discuss the different levels with examples from your setting. In Exercise 11, the role-playing similarly should reflect issues in the participants' environment.

Using experiences adapted to your groups' needs, together with the systematic stage-by-stage process, will ensure maximum effectiveness. The first task is to help participants open the perceptual door and take off the blinders they often wear. Once they can begin to identify racism in institutions, the culture, and themselves, they can expand that awareness. Therefore, the specific focus that is used—school, business, academic community, and so on—becomes less important than developing the understanding of the underlying dimensions of racism. The setting is essentially a vehicle through which to develop that awareness.

Formats

The program has been used in various formats, ranging from three-hour introductory sessions to semester-long university courses to three-day intensive education in corporations. Often all that can be provided within the time limits are short introductory sessions. I have facilitated three-hour segments that concentrate on Stage 1 concepts. These can provide a means for some to begin to explore their attitudes. It is usually a door opener, no more. I have often experienced a high degree of personal frustration in such sessions. If you can be clear and realistic about goals—that is, be content to raise the issue of racism and help participants begin to explore it—you will probably lessen your own frustration. When you are using Stage 1 experiences only, it is essential to go slowly and avoid making participants defensive. That is a difficult task in a short, onetime workshop. The hope is that you can create enough concern that the participants will continue to probe the issue on their own.

One-day, eight-hour sessions can be expanded to include institutional issues in Stage 2 and some strategy planning in Stage 6. One popular design, which has been used with in-service and preservice teachers, includes Exercises 3, 6, and 7 (Stage 1); 9, 14, and 18 (Stage 2); and 43 and 46 (Stage 6). These exercises help to establish definitions, give teachers some awareness of institutional racism in the educational process, and help them to develop ways to use that learning in their classrooms. The more time you have, of course, the more effective your program will be. More exercises have been included than can probably be used in any one workshop.

Although times are suggested for each exercise, these are approximations only, and many can be shorter or longer, depending on how participants respond and how involved they become. No matter what combination of exercises you use, it is important to follow the systematic process. It is important to consider the level of sophistication and experience of your group. You may need to spend only a short time on Stages 1 and 2 and concentrate on the remaining stages. You should know your group and identify what will fit their level of awareness without making too many assumptions that they truly understand racism and its manifestations simply because they have volunteered take part. Remember that the foundation built in Stages 1 and 2 is critical to developing a shared group perspective for the work in the later stages.

In developing your design, allow time for your participants to reflect on and integrate the materials and concepts. I often provide Stage 1 reading materials before beginning the program. In this way participants can begin to think and raise questions.

Finally, plan for follow-up sessions. The more reinforcement participants have, the more they may be able to change. It is difficult to become anti-racist in a racist system. Your participants will need support to make changes in and around themselves. Structure that reinforcement into the design and impress on the participants the need to develop a new support system that will help them to learn and continue to grow with respect to becoming an anti-racist. Ongoing task forces and support groups often develop as a result.

Measuring Program Effectiveness

One of the problems involved in any form of training or education is determining its effectiveness. A question often asked particularly of racism training is, Are white people really changing, or are they merely becoming more knowledgeable racists? I am convinced that awareness is not enough. It is behavior that counts. My charge to the user of this program is to impress on participants the importance of changing not merely attitudes but also behavior. Stokely Carmichael's adage, "If you're not part of the solution, you're part of the problem," still holds, as does the adage, inaction is action.

If participants are involved six months later in some positive new behavior, I consider the program effective. In the school setting, such behavior can range from teaching short courses or offering workshops to changing curricula to reflect a multicultural perspective.

When measuring the degree of effectiveness of the program, I have used such instruments as the Steckler Anti-Black and Anti-White Scales (Steckler, 1957) and the Attitude Exploration Survey (Adams, 1973) to assess attitude change and the Behavioral Rating Scale (Uhlemann, 1968) to measure behavior change. On these scales, as well as the subjective evaluations of leaders and participants, the program is demonstrably successful. Whatever means are used, it is essential that we evaluate both the participants' growth and the facilitator's effectiveness.

A Final Note

In dealing with racism, keep in mind its complexity, its pervasiveness, and its entrenchment in white society. Change often comes slowly. Par-

32

ticipants may leave the program with little or no apparent changes in their perspectives but in time begin to see racism and themselves in a new light. The process of developing awareness, accepting and owning one's whiteness, and developing ways to change is difficult. The facilitator's job is to help whites take the first steps in that process.

PART TWO   **The Training Program**

Stage 1   **Racism: Definitions and Inconsistencies**

Stage 1   Racism: Definitions and Inconsistencies

Stage 1 is a crucial step in the reeducation of white people. It lays the groundwork for participants to explore racism in society and in themselves. To achieve this end, it is necessary to

1. Help people feel comfortable in the group, get to know one another, and develop trust.
2. Help individuals discover and define key terminology basic to understanding the dynamics of racism.
3. Help name and begin exploring inconsistencies in society.

All the exercises in this stage have been developed to meet these objectives.

Given the objectives, Stage 1 seems a formidable challenge. Participants usually enter this stage with different levels of awareness as a result of their assumptions, perceptions, and personal experiences with racism. It is necessary to meet them where they are, as well as to develop an atmosphere that ensures that they can work together as a group. Stage 1 helps participants get to know one another and feel comfortable. In the initial warm-up activities they share their perspectives in order to develop a climate of commonality.

Rationale

The defining process is one of the most important steps in understanding racism. Many participants use the words *bias, bigotry, prejudice,* and *racism* interchangeably. It is vital to clearly define each of these terms so that participants can distinguish among them and have a common language. In this way they will have the necessary basis for exploring racism and the way it operates in U.S. society. Many of the exercises in Stage 1 focus on the defining process to facilitate the further exploration of institutional, cultural, and individual racism in later stages.

It is also important that participants look at their own beliefs, attitudes, and values and see how they act on them. Another part of this stage is thus designed to highlight inconsistencies between words and actions.

Because it is easier at first to look outside ourselves when dealing with racism, inconsistencies are explored in terms of the society's values and attitudes, which are then compared with actual behavior. This survey lays the groundwork for later stages, in which participants explore their own ideologies and behaviors for inconsistencies.

The participants explore fundamental U.S. ideologies such as All people are created equal; America is a land of equal opportunity; You can make it if you try; and Liberty and justice for all. Then they confront the fact that these beliefs are not matched by actions. This learning is basic to an awareness of the "American dilemma" described by Myrdal (1944).This stage names this dilemma. Awareness of inconsistencies is then further developed in each subsequent stage as a crucial aspect of each participant's education.

Method

As a facilitator you will be working on three levels. This makes your task very different from, and perhaps more difficult than, leading a nonspecific issue-oriented group, such as a T-group. In this particular group you will need to deal with

1. The climate of the group.
2. Content vis-à-vis racism.
3. Your own issues of racism.

It is important to be aware that this is probably the first time this group has come together to deal with the issues of racism in a structured environment. Therefore, the facilitator must be sensitive to issues in a "new group" as well as to the content of the program. It is necessary to develop trust and a supportive climate. One way to accomplish this is through the initial exercises in Stage 1. Another way is through the support of the facilitator. That support might include *not* processing racist language and remarks throughout Stage 1. Clearly, on the issue of racism people will be unwilling to share their real, innermost feelings and attitudes if they do not feel the support of the group and the facilitator and if they do not perceive that the environment is safe. By processing participants' racism in Stage 1, the facilitator may shut them down. Racist remarks and language, such as discussion of "reverse racism," racist jokes, or expressions such as "blacklisting" and "black sheep," should be noted and processed at a point when the participants can hear the comments and understand them. What is important in this first stage is that the facilitator begin to develop a climate of trust and safety. The degree of rapport that the facilitator has with the group, as well as the feeling in the group itself, will either help or hinder the learning of the participants.

A second aspect of facilitating the group pertains to content. The first stage concentrates on external issues: participants are engaged intellectually in exploring definitional and societal inconsistencies. They are steered away from exploring personal racism, because at the outset it is easier to look at issues outside themselves.

Another Stage 1 dynamic related directly to the issue of racism is the participants' questions about how they can deal with racism in an all-white group. Here the facilitator must take an active role (if no one else in the group does) and point out that many white people have developed racist attitudes without having had any contact (positive or negative) with people of color and that, therefore, through various mechanisms the participants can explore their racism without the presence of people of color. The facilitator should emphasize that in many anti-racism training programs people of color are exploited. White people learn from them about racism—but what do the people of color learn? The question becomes, who would benefit if the group were mixed, and at whose expense?

In this stage—and in succeeding ones as well—the facilitator must take an active role. In Stage 1 that role includes pressing for understanding and acceptance of the definitions of racism and prejudice.

The third, and perhaps most difficult, task of the facilitator involves your own role in the process. You should be knowledgeable about dealing with racism as a white problem. That includes being aware of your racism, understanding the process of racism, and being committed to continuing to learn about your own racism. It is crucial that you discuss this with the group, making it clear that in fact you are not *the* expert on racism and moreover cannot speak for people of color. Your role as facilitator is to help other white people begin to understand what racism is and to find ways to combat it. Ideally, this is a continuous process for all members of the group. The facilitator thus has the complex task of not only facilitating participants' growth and development but also remaining open to your own learning.

The content and process issues summarized above are the basis for Stage 1 and ultimately for all stages in the program. The pages that follow set forth the specific mechanisms, exercises, and resources necessary for the development of the first stage.

Exercise 1   Establishing Goals and Objectives

Goals

1. To help participants feel comfortable in the group.
2. To understand participants' expectations.

**Materials
Needed**

None

Instructions

1. Have the group sit in a circle. (To encourage openness, it is best to not have tables in the room or for the facilitator to sit behind a table.)
2. Ask the participants to share
   a. Their names.
   b. Their reasons for participating in the workshop.
   c. Their expectations of the workshop and anticipated learning.
3. Share your (the facilitator's) own expectations for the workshop:
   a. Participants will take responsibility for their own learning.
   b. Participants will share their feelings and be as honest as possible.
   c. For learning to occur, we need to create a safe environment and to be willing to lean into discomfort.

**Note to
Facilitator**

Any form of expectation-sharing exercise would be useful. You may want to begin with an experience that serves to get people acquainted and then follow with a separate experience to share expectations.

Time

10 to 15 minutes (all times noted apply to groups of twelve to fifteen persons)

Exercise 2   Concentric Circles: Getting to Know One Another

1. To help participants begin to raise the issue of racism. **Goals**
2. To begin developing a climate of trust, safety, and support.

None **Materials Needed**

1. Have the group count off by twos (*1-2-1-2*). **Instructions**
2. a. Ask all the "1s" to sit in a circle with their backs to the center of the circle.
   b. Ask all the "2s" to sit in an outside circle, facing the "1s" (each person has a partner facing her or him).
3. Ask all the "1s" to share with the person opposite them
   a. Their names.
   b. "Something special that happened to me this week."
   (This process should continue for about two minutes.)
4. Ask all the "2s" to repeat the same process.
5. Ask all the "2s" to move one person to the right.
6. Have them repeat the above process, sharing names and responding to "One feeling I have about being here."
7. Continue this process for another two to four rounds, always asking the "2s" to move one person to the right. Other exchanges that may be asked for include
   a. "Share the first word that comes to your mind when you think about racism."
   b. "Share one experience you have had with racism and how you responded."
   c. "Share one feeling you have about dealing with racism."
   d. "Share why you believe whites need to address racism."

Adapted from an exercise developed by Gerald Weinstein, School of Education, University of Massachusetts.

It is important to be alert to the issues that participants bring to the group. Particularly observe the questions that deal specifically with racism.

Time   20 to 30 minutes

Exercise 3   Definition of Prejudice

1. To help participants begin to understand prejudice.   **Goals**
2. To develop a functional definition of prejudice.

Materials
Prejudice Definition Sheet (p. 45)   **Needed**
Easel paper
Markers
Masking tape

1. Begin the activity by stating that it is essential to understand the dif-   **Instructions**
   ference between racism and prejudice before exploring how they
   operate in our society. Then begin to explore the definitions of prejudice.
2. Pass out copies of the Prejudice Definition Sheet.
3. Ask the participants to look at the four definitions presented on the
   sheet. Using the four as a starting point, ask each person to develop
   a definition of prejudice with which she or he feels comfortable.
4. Divide the group into small groups of four.
5. Ask the participants to share their individual definitions in the small
   groups and then develop a group definition of prejudice. Ask someone in each group to jot down the definition on the easel paper.
6. After fifteen minutes ask each group to hang up its easel paper and
   share its definitions with the large group.
7. Reactions, discussion. Points raised should include the following:
   a. Prejudice is based on assumptions that have not been checked
      out.
   b. The word *prejudice* is composed of *pre* and *judge*. This is a key
      concept in understanding prejudice.
   c. It is important to understand the difference between prejudice and
      bias.

This exercise begins to highlight the key dynamics of prejudice and begins distinguishing prejudice from racism. You may want to include a mini-lecture on the differences between prejudice and bias. A good resource is Pat Bidol, "Mini-Lecture on the Difference Between Prejudice and Racism" (see Resource List).

Time   25 minutes

Prejudice Definition Sheet

In the *American Heritage Dictionary* (2000), *prejudice* is defined as

1. a. An adverse judgment or opinion formed beforehand or without knowledge or examination of the facts; b. A preconceived preference or idea.
2. The act or state of holding unreasonable preconceived judgments or convictions.
3. Irrational suspicion or hatred of a particular group, race, or religion.
4. Detriment or injury caused to a person by the preconceived, unfavorable conviction of another or others.

Exercise 4   Exploring Prejudice: *The Lunch Date*

Goal

To further define prejudice and how it functions.

**Materials
Needed**

The Lunch Date (video)
TV
VCR

Instructions

1. Show the video *The Lunch Date*.
2. Stop the video halfway through. Ask the participants to share what they have observed and the assumptions made by themselves and by those in the video.
3. Ask the participants to predict what will happen next.
4. Show the rest of the video.
5. Reactions, discussion. Questions raised should include
   a. How do we stereotype each other?
   b. How do our assumptions and preconceived ideas about one another foster prejudice?
6. Ask the participants to brainstorm specific examples of prejudiced behavior.
7. Ask the participants to discuss what assumptions each character might have been making about the other.

Time

30 minutes (video is 11 minutes)

Exercise 5   Designing a Racist Community

1. To identify the key elements of racism.   **Goals**
2. To discover how racism functions in our society.

Easel paper   **Materials**
Markers   **Needed**
Masking tape

1. Divide the participants into groups of four to six persons. Give each   **Instructions**
   group easel paper and markers.
2. Ask the groups to design a racist community or organization. Have
   each group describe its community or organization on the paper. It
   can be blatantly or subtly racist. Ask the groups to make sure they
   describe
   a. The makeup of the community or organization.
   b. Who makes decisions.
   c. How the decisions are made.
   d. Who has control of money.
   e. Who establishes the formal policy of the community or organiza-
      tion.
   f. Who establishes the informal policy of the community or organi-
      zation.
   g. The roles of the various institutions of the community—schools,
      churches, businesses, media, social organizations, recreational
      facilities *or* the various structures of the organization—and the
      roles that individuals and groups play.
3. Post the papers and ask each group to share its community or organization with the whole group.

Design created by Duke Harris, Pat Bidol, and Dan Kirchbaum.

4. Reactions, discussion. Points raised should include the following:
   a. What are the key elements that make your community or organization and others racist? List these elements separately on a sheet of paper headed "Racism Is . . . " (this list will be used in Exercise 9).
   b. How different is your community or organization from real communities or organizations in the United States?
   c. Review the elements the groups listed in their designs of a racist community. Focus on the power issues: whites have the power to oppress people of color in this country, but people of color do not have the power to oppress whites.

Note to Facilitator

1. This is one of the most important activities of this series. It generates a lot of data that you will be using constantly throughout this stage and the succeeding stages.
2. Before proceeding, you should discuss the importance of this exercise. Emphasize that it is necessary to be aware of and able to pinpoint clearly what racism is—that is, how it functions—before we can begin to combat it. We must know exactly what we are trying to fight in order to fight it effectively. And it is important to understand the scope of how racism operates so that the strategies developed are substantive and can adequately effect change.
3. During the exercise, you should move from group to group to observe the process and to hear the discussion. It may be helpful to keep a record of individuals' ideologies to discuss with them at a later point in the workshop.
4. During the exercise, there is often a tendency for participants to try to make people of color the oppressors by putting them in the majority and reversing the actual roles people take in our society. It is extremely important to note this in processing the exercise: Why do people try to deny the role of whites in this country? Does this really happen in the United States? If so, how? What kind of power do people of color have in this country? Where does it exist? It is essential that participants begin to look at their ownership of and responsibility for racism. This exercise begins to clarify the reality that whites are responsible for racism and that we need to look at the systemic and institutional impacts that racism has on people of color. It is often too easy for whites to discuss the individual or interpersonal impact of racism (and thereby discuss how we may feel discriminated against) rather than examine and take responsibility for the

48

ways in which institutional, systemic, and cultural racism advantages whites as a group and as individuals.

5. This exercise also helps participants to begin exploring inconsistencies in U.S. society. The behaviors listed on the sheet entitled "Racism Is . . . " will prove helpful in Exercise 9, "Naming and Discovering Inconsistencies."

2 hours (1 hour for group work, 1 hour to process) **Time**

Exercise 6   Fuzzy Concept: Racism

Goals   To clarify further the elements of racism.

Materials   Easel paper
Needed   Pens and pencils (or markers)

Instructions   1. Ask the participants to draw a circle on easel paper with lines radi-
                         ating from it.
                      2. In the middle of the circle write the word *racism.*
                      3. Ask the participants to free-associate with the word *racism* and write
                         their responses at the end of each line.
                      4. Share the circles in the large group.

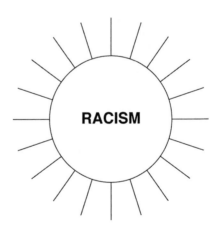

Time   15 to 20 minutes

Exercise 7   Definition of Racism

Goals

1. To develop a functional definition of racism.
2. To clarify the differences between racism and prejudice.

**Materials
Needed**

Racism Definition Sheet (p. 53)
Easel paper
Markers
Masking tape

Instructions

1. Hand out copies of the Racism Definition Sheet.
2. Ask the participants to look at the three definitions presented on the sheet. Using them as a starting point, ask the participants to discuss and develop their own definitions of racism.
3. Divide the group into groups of four.
4. Ask the participants to share their individual definitions in the small groups and then develop a group definition of racism. Ask someone in the group to write the definition on the easel paper.
5. After fifteen minutes ask each group to display its definition and share it with the large group.
6. Reactions, discussion. Points raised should include the following:
   a. What seems to be common to all the definitions?
   b. Is power part of your group's definition? If not, how does your definition differ from prejudice?
   c. What is power, and how do you define it (in institutional, political, or economic terms)?
   d. Who has the power in our society? (If necessary, refer to the racist communities/organizations designed in Exercise 5).
   e. By the definition of racism, are people of color in the United States today racist against whites?
   f. Do people of color currently have the power to oppress whites as a group?

1. Refer again to the definition of prejudice and differentiate it from racism. By the end of this exercise these two terms should have distinct meanings for the participants.
2. It is important to push for the understanding that racism is *prejudice plus power* and therefore people of color cannot be racist against whites in the United States. People of color can be prejudiced against whites but clearly do not have the power as a group to enforce that prejudice. Although participants may not, at this point, totally accept this view or feel comfortable with it, it is important to establish the concept as a working definition. As the course progresses, it will be better understood by participants.

Time   30 minutes

Racism Definition Sheet

In the *American Heritage Dictionary* (2000), *racism* is defined as

1. The belief that race accounts for differences in human character or ability and that a particular race is superior to others.
2. Discrimination or prejudice based on race.

To these definitions may be added

3. Prejudice plus power.

Stage 2   Confronting the Reality of Racism

Stage 2   Confronting the Reality of Racism

The focus of Stage 1 was developing an understanding of prejudice and **Introduction**
racism by establishing clear definitions. Stage 2 elaborates on the definition of racism by exploring the specifics of institutional racism. The
exercises in this second stage are designed to

1. Confront participants with institutional racism.
2. Begin to reeducate participants about the functioning of racism in
   institutions.
3. Highlight inconsistencies between institutional values and attitudes
   and institutional behaviors.

So that participants will comprehend that racism is a predominantly   **Rationale**
white problem, they must be challenged with and become aware of the
depth and breadth of racism in U.S. institutions and society. Stage 2 seeks
to explore in detail how deeply racism is ingrained in every aspect of our
lives, how it exists in us as individuals from birth onward, and how it
operates in every institutional system.

   The exercises in this section are extremely diverse. Some of the exercises permit participants to experience oppression, on a very small
scale, through simulation. Others expose participants to the perspectives of people of color who have experienced the effects of racism. Still
others illustrate how white people benefit from institutional racism, as
well as how we are trapped by it. Participants will also be engaged in
discovering for themselves how institutional racism functions. Each
exercise contains one essential element, a focus on inconsistencies. It
is essential to point out the inconsistencies between the values and attitudes of U.S. institutions and their actual behavior. Once we can see the
discrepancies between the two, we can better determine the positive
steps that need to be taken to close the gaps.

   In Stage 2 many crucial issues are explored. This stage further clari-
fies and expands on the functional definitions developed in Stage 1.
Stage 2 is concerned with exploring in-depth the American dilemma:
our institutions' espoused values of equality, meritocracy, and a level

playing field juxtaposed to the reality of racism and the use of power and privilege that keeps whites at an advantage. Through Stage 2 participants begin to understand how racism manifests itself in ways that blame the victim and work to negate the role of whites in perpetuating and supporting racism. Participants learn that on an institutional level "reverse racism" does not exist in the United States today.

Method

Stage 2 presents a number of challenges to the facilitator. It can be an extremely emotional stage for participants. They may find themselves feeling confused, overwhelmed, unprepared to deal with all the new data. It is important to keep these feelings at a manageable level but not to discharge them completely. In Stage 3 all these feelings will be intensified. One way to manage reactions of denial, resistance, and feelings of guilt is to emphasize that racism is deeply ingrained in our system and that we are clearly products of our system. Thus it should not come as a surprise that we as white people are racist. The question will become, at a later stage, what can we do about it?

An important dynamic to try to achieve in the group during this stage is ownership of racism as a white problem and ownership of the effect of racism on people of color, including some acceptance of responsibility to make changes in the system to overcome it.

It is also crucial to focus on white people's behavior. The group may often attempt to change the focus of the discussion to identify instances and systems of "racism" among people of color directed at whites ("reverse racism"). It is important to process this reaction and discuss the group's need for flight from some of the real issues of racism in U.S. society and from a close look at the American system as a whole, in which white racism is pervasive.

It is important for the facilitator to challenge long-held beliefs and assumptions in this stage. Your job is to highlight hard realities about institutional racism and at the same time avoid attacking participants as individuals. It is an especially difficult challenge to get participants to look at systemic dynamics because there is a tendency in white culture to see the world through an individual lens. In Stage 2 participants are being asked to see the world in a new way. In this stage participants are challenged to begin to examine the institutions that nurtured their development.

Exercise 8   Mini-Lecture: Kinds and Levels of Racism

1. To deepen participants' understanding of the definition of racism developed in Stage 1 by pinpointing the different kinds and levels of racism.   **Goals**
2. To move participants from Stage 1 to Stage 2, which is concerned with exploring institutional racism.

Chart below on easel paper (or chalkboard)   **Materials**
Masking tape   **Needed**

1. The following chart can serve as a guide in discussing the different kinds and levels of racism. Display it and refer to it while giving the mini-lecture.   **Instructions**

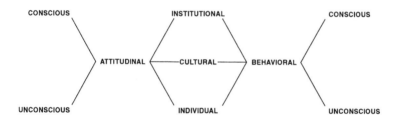

2. Follow the outline below in developing the mini-lecture.

I. Kinds of Racism
  A. Institutional
    1. Education
    2. Economics
    3. Health services
    4. Politics
    5. Housing
    6. Judicial system

B. Cultural
1. Values, beliefs
2. Communication
3. Standards, needs, norms
4. Family structure
5. Aesthetics
6. Language
7. Holidays/traditions
8. Art
9. Food
10. Dress
11. Music/dance
12. Games

C. Individual
1. Attitudes
2. Behaviors
3. Socialization
4. Self-interest
5. Interaction
6. Communication
7. Expression of emotion

II. Levels of Racism
A. Conscious level
1. Institutional racist attitudes
a. Belief in limited intellectual abilities of children of color
b. Belief in stereotypes shown in media
c. Belief that affirmative action is reverse racism
d. Belief that people of color are less qualified
2. Institutional racist behaviors
a. Discrimination against people of color in housing
b. Voucher systems/charter schools
c. Use of quota systems; tokenism
d. Racial profiling
e. Disparities in judicial system
f. Anti-immigration efforts
3. Individual racist attitudes
a. Belief that whites deserve their privilege and advantage

    b. Belief that people of color deserve their position in society and that with hard work they can succeed like whites

    c. Belief that Native Americans are alcoholics

  4. Individual racist behaviors

    a. Bombing of black churches; lynching of black people

    b. Use of racial slurs ("nigger"); nooses on people's desks

    c. Support of Confederate flag as "historical"

    d. "English-only" movement

B. Unconscious level

  1. Institutional racist attitudes

    a. Assumptions that white people can meet the needs of all the people in the institution but that staff members of color can deal only with the needs of other people of color

    b. Disregard the needs of people of color in developing products and services (e.g., "flesh-colored" Band-Aids, which reflect whites' color)

    c. Disregard the perspectives of people of color or the need for unbiased content in standardized tests and using such tests as measures of "intelligence"

  2. Institutional racist behaviors

    a. Destruction of housing occupied by people of color in urban renewal to make way for commercial facilities or upper-income housing

    b. Teaching of white history as American history

    c. Denial of health benefits and access to adequate coverage to illegal immigrants and other people of color

    d. Not giving honest and direct feedback to people of color

  3. Individual racist attitudes

    a. Belief in melting pot theory

    b. Denial of racism, insistence on being color blind ("When I see black people, I don't see their color. People are people.")

    c. Belief that all people are treated equally in the United States

    d. Belief in a meritocracy and a level playing field

  4. Individual racist behavior

    a. Laughing at racist jokes

    b. Collusion of silence—witnessing racism in action and doing nothing

c. Dealing with companies who have poor records for diversity and equality

d. Use of anti-black, pro-white language (e.g., "black lie," "white lie")

e. Excluding people of color from your inner circle or relegating them to certain roles, such as support staff or housekeepers

Close the mini-lecture by pointing out that these examples of kinds and levels of racism are but a few illustrations and that others will be identified in subsequent sessions. Emphasize that racism need not be intentional but that by their very support of racist institutions and cultural mores whites are helping to perpetuate the racist system. Ask participants to share their examples and add to the list.

Note to Facilitator

1. This exercise is useful as a bridge from Stage 1 to Stage 2. At the end of Stage 1 participants may feel lost about where to begin exploring racism. Now that they have defined racism and have gained some awareness of its pervasiveness, the next step is to begin exploring the dynamics of racism. This mini-lecture presents racism in manageable segments. It also helps to minimize any anxiety in the group. By discussing racism in terms of kinds and levels, participants usually become open to the issues presented in Stage 2. They see that their exploration will continue to be restricted to areas outside of themselves; institutions, not their own behavior, will be investigated. At this stage participants find it easier to look at institutions for racism than to explore their own attitudes and behavior.

2. In the development of this mini-lecture the following reading from Stage 1 is useful: "Mini-Lecture: Differences Between Prejudice and Racism."

3. This exercise should be short. Specifics of each kind of racism will unfold in subsequent sessions.

4. If the setting of the group is an educational institution, it might be useful to administer the test discussed in Exercise 21 before conducting this exercise.

Time   15 to 20 minutes

Exercise 9   Naming and Discovering Inconsistencies: An "American" Dilemma

To explore inconsistencies in society's ideology and behavior.   **Goals**

Easel paper   **Materials**
Markers   **Needed**
Masking tape
Sheet "Racism Is . . . " developed in Exercise 5

1. Divide group into groups of four to six persons.   **Instructions**
2. Ask each group to brainstorm a list of ideologies and slogans ("All people are created equal," "Liberty and justice for all," etc.) that the United States professes as part of its basic philosophy. Have them write them on easel paper.
3. Ask each group to share its list.
4. In the large group ask the participants to name examples of areas in which these ideologies are true. You may want to add ideologies they omitted (see "Commonly Listed Ideologies and Slogans," p. 62).
5. Discuss the implications of inconsistencies and the American dilemma.
6. Use the sheet "Racism Is . . . ," developed in Exercise 5, to sum up inconsistencies in American ideology and behavior. Discuss how those inconsistencies foster and perpetuate racism.

This is one of the first exercises in the series dealing specifically with   **Note to**
inconsistencies or discrepancies between our ideology of opportunity   **Facilitator**
and the reality of oppression. Because it is a crucial concept in the
development of the workshop, you may wish to ask participants to
keep a journal, noting inconsistencies that they become aware of in
society and in themselves.

35 minutes   **Time**

Commonly Listed Ideologies and Slogans

Pull yourself up by your bootstraps.
You can make it if you try.
God created man [sic] in his own image.
To get a good job, first get a good education.
First come, first served.
Freedom of the press, freedom of speech.
Do unto others as they have done unto you.
Cleanliness is next to godliness.
Government of the people, by the people, for the people.
Free enterprise.
Hard work will equal success.
From rags to riches.
All men are created equal.
Liberty and justice for all.
Land of the free, home of the brave.
In God we trust.
The American dream.
America, the melting pot.
Live free or die (New Hampshire license plate).
Rights guaranteed under the law.
From sea to shining sea (manifest destiny).
One nation under God.
It's a level playing field.
America is a meritocracy.

Exercise 10   The Web of Institutional Racism: A Simulation Game

Goals

1. To help participants begin to understand some of the dynamics of institutional racism by experiencing, on a small scale, how racism oppresses people of color.
2. To help participants begin to understand the power behind white racism.

Materials Needed

Four staff persons to run the institutions of the simulation: the bank, the university, the employment agency, and the real estate office
Signs for each institution
Play money
Goal sheets for participants
Housing cards
Employment cards
Forms for each institution
Instruction manual for simulation

Instructions

This simulation requires a minimum of eighteen participants to be fully effective. At the start of the simulation each participant is given a specific role and a goal that she or he must try to achieve within the six years of the game (each round represents a year). These roles reflect the positions of people of color in U.S. society today. All the goals revolve around participants' interactions with the four institutions.

Each institution is operated by a member of the board of directors. This board is responsible for setting up the standards and policies of each institution. In the end the board has the power to decide who makes it under the standards and policies it develops. Participants attempt to meet their goals—such as moving into better homes or apartments, getting better jobs, and starting businesses—and find themselves exposed to a system that is frustrating, selective in determining who receives benefits and gets ahead, and generally oppressive in its treatment of people.

Simulation game designed by Carole and Charles Camp.

Some participants meet obstacle after obstacle trying to reach their goals while others get full cooperation from the system. As a result participants experience the injustice of the system, and particularly the power that is a basic ingredient of racism. They begin to realize through their own experiences how power can work to maintain the advantage of one group over another. They personally experience a taste of the frustration and anger that is a part of the everyday lives of many people of color.

As a result of these feelings participants will sometimes try to take over or overthrow the institutions, rob the bank, form a new system, or join together. They often gain an understanding of violence (destruction of both property and individual integrity) that sometimes occurs as a result of being blocked by the system.

The simulation provides a valuable mechanism for participants not only to learn about how institutional racism functions but also to experience on a very small scale some of the dynamics of racism and the effects it has on the lives of people of color. Through the simulation participants can get in touch with their own racism and perhaps question some of their values, as well as examine overt and covert aspects of institutional racism.

Note to Facilitator	If it is not feasible to do this simulation, Exercise 11, "Institutional Racism at Work: A Simulation Experience," addresses many of the same issues.
Time	3 hours

Exercise 11   Institutional Racism at Work:
A Simulation Experience

1. To help participants begin to understand some of the dynamics of institutional racism by experiencing how racism oppresses people. **Goals**
2. To help participants begin to understand the power in white racism.

Simulation Design 1: College Setting (p. 67)   **Materials**
Simulation Design 2: Public School Setting (p. 69)   **Needed**

1. Assign roles to participants (at least thirteen people are required for Simulation Design 1, eleven for Simulation Design 2). You may assign each person's role or let participants choose their roles. **Instructions**
2. Hand out role slips. Read the description of the situation so that the setting is clear to the group.
3. Have the groups meet for five minutes to plan their strategies and assess their positions.
4. Call the groups together for the meeting. The facilitator serves as process observer.
5. Continue the simulation for about forty minutes.
6. Process: Ask the participants to share how they felt in their roles. Then share your process notes with the group.

1. You may wish to choose the people who role-play people of color, selecting those participants who strongly resist accepting the definition of racism or who have trouble understanding why people of color need and/or want to maintain their own cultural identities. **Note to** **Facilitator**
2. In sharing your process observations, be as specific as possible in noting what people say. Pay close attention to language ("you people," "they," "them"). Also take note of those who show their support for people of color. Focus on the reactions of the participants playing people of color. Are they realistic? How do they feel in those

This simulation may be substituted for Exercise 10.

roles? Are they self-conscious, overstereotyping, empathetic? Also, it is important to focus on how those playing whites felt in their roles: were they self-conscious? aware? cautious? Did they work to bridge the situation?

3. Be sure to leave ample time to process so that participants are not left hanging with their feelings.

Time   1 hour 30 minutes (5 minutes for group meetings, 40 minutes for simulation, 30–45 minutes for processing)

Simulation Design 1: College Setting

The setting is an all-white residence hall. It is late spring, near the end of term. The head of residence will be staying on the next year, and all the counselors for the next year have been chosen.

The residence hall has a stated commitment to deal with racism. A group of students of color has been approached by the head of residence to discuss the possibility that some might move into the residence hall. To date no official meetings have taken place to put this into effect. You will all meet to discuss the issues involved.

HEAD OF RESIDENCE

You are a white head of residence who has worked hard in your residence hall to address racism. Now there is support from some students to have people of color move into the building. You have been in touch with their student representatives and have some knowledge of their needs. In your position you have the responsibility to meet with the students in your residence hall, the counselors, and the students of color to make sure that any actions taken are productive for all concerned.

RESIDENCE ADVISORS (4)

You are members of an all-white staff in an all-white residence hall. As a staff member you have stated your agreement with the residence hall's goals of combating racism. Some residents of your floors are concerned about the possibility of a group of students of color moving into the hall. None of you is certain yet how this will affect your own floor, if at all. To date you are not sure what needs and concerns the students of color have. You are to meet as a group to discuss the issue.

WHITE STUDENTS A (2)

You have taken a sociology course on race relations. You are concerned about not having a full educational experience because you live in an all-white residence hall. You represent an ad hoc group of students who formed when they heard that a large number of students of color might move into the residence hall.

67

WHITE STUDENTS B (2)

You represent a group of seniors who have lived in the residence hall for four years. You are concerned about a number of students of color moving into the residence hall. You are afraid that these students might use residence hall dues in an inequitable way and are also concerned about changing the all-white makeup of the residence hall. You feel that there is no need for special treatment of students of color and that if they want to live in the residence hall, they can follow the usual housing procedures.

STUDENTS OF COLOR (4)

A number of students of color have agreed to move into the residence hall, provided that their needs and concerns are met. You represent these students and their concerns, which include the following:

1. Residence hall activities must be geared to their needs. You feel that this can best be accomplished by allocating a specific proportion of residence hall dues to students of color who will be living in the residence hall and letting you decide how to spend the money for the activities you want.
2. All students of color want to live together rather than dispersed throughout the residence hall. You also want a counselor of color on the floor.
3. You want equal representation on the residence hall council in order to play an active role in policy making.
4. You do not want to be exploited for the benefit of white students' awareness of racism.

Simulation Design 2: Public School Setting

Nathaniel Hawthorne Middle School is a predominantly white public school. Of the seven hundred students, seventy-five are black and Native American.

Recently there was an incident between two students. A white male student called a black male student "nigger" and a fight ensued. This incident stirred up many feelings among the black and Native American students. They put together a list of demands to present to the administration. At the request of the students of color, the principal has called a meeting with representatives of the students of color, counselors, teachers, and white students to discuss the issues.

PRINCIPAL

You are a white principal, age forty-five. As the principal for the past ten years, you have established rapport with your staff and students. You have a reputation for being sensitive and fair to all students in your school. You are extremely concerned about this incident and astonished that racial issues exist in the school. Since so few students of color attend the school, you had never seen a problem there.

As principal you have the responsibility to call a meeting with the representatives of counselors, teachers, and students. Your goal is to make sure that the actions taken are productive for all concerned and in the best interests of the school.

COUNSELOR A

You are a white counselor who has been at Nathaniel Hawthorne Middle School for seven years. Your major responsibility is maintenance of students' records and administration of IQ tests. You believe that IQ tests are important indicators of students' success in the academic system.

COUNSELOR B

You are a white counselor who has been at Nathaniel Hawthorne Middle School for two and a half years. You have a real concern for the kids at the school and seem to be well liked. In your role you see yourself

69

as really trying to help kids, and many come to you with their personal problems.

TEACHER A
You are a white teacher. You are very active in the fight for social justice and belong to several political groups who have demonstrated and petitioned the government for more equality among the races. You strongly believe that people are people and you pride yourself on being color blind.

TEACHER B
You are a white teacher. You have strong Christian beliefs. Your basic philosophy has been to turn the other cheek whenever conflict occurs. According to your religious philosophy, all people are part of the "brotherhood of man."

TEACHER C
You are a white teacher. You have taught at Nathaniel Hawthorne Middle School for twenty years. In fact, the parents of some of the students now in your classes were students of yours.

TEACHER D
You are a white teacher. This is your first year at Nathaniel Hawthorne Middle School.

WHITE STUDENT A
You are very concerned about the racial incident and the unrest in the school. You represent an ad hoc group that formed on hearing about the incident. Some of your friends are black, and they socialize with you. Your group formed to support the students of color.

WHITE STUDENT B
You are one of a group of white students who banded together when you heard about the incident. You are a friend of the white student who was involved, and you are very angry about the whole situation. You feel that students of color are just too sensitive and need to realize that the kid didn't mean any harm by his name calling.

STUDENTS OF COLOR (2)
The incident between the white and black students was the straw that broke the camel's back. As a result of the incident you have worked out

70

a list of demands to the school that are *nonnegotiable.* You will not be coerced or co-opted. You have legal connections and if necessary will sue the school for the cruel and abusive treatment, as well as for failure to get what you need in the way of an education. Your grievances and demands include the following:

1. You are tired of the attitudes in school. You are tired of being humiliated and insulted daily by name-calling teachers and students—overt and covert ("nigger," "colored," "savage").
2. You want an end to the all-white curriculum and all-white textbooks. Only white history is taught. There must be more to history than blacks as slaves or Native Americans as savages. You are tired of tokenism, such as Black History Month. No Native American history is taught. Is Native American history nonexistent? In literature classes the only novels read are white novels.
3. You refuse to take any more IQ tests. You feel that they are discriminatory and should not be given at all. You are calling for an end to all IQ testing in the school.
4. The school is to do away with the Pledge of Allegiance in the mornings until there is freedom and justice for all.
5. Thanksgiving Day should be made a day of mourning. Malcolm X's birthday should be a day off.
6. You want black and Native American teachers and counselors. You feel that the white teachers and counselors are not meeting your needs. Teachers' expectations and attitudes toward you are negative. Counselors merely push you into sports and nonacademic areas.
7. You are tired of being exploited. Whenever an issue involving blacks or Native Americans comes up, you are asked to tell whites what it's like to be black or Native American. Otherwise you are invisible.
8. You want an equal number of representatives on the student council. The total number of representatives is twelve. You want six seats for students of color.

Exercise 12   "The Drawbridge"

Goals

1. To explore individual values connected with institutional racism.
2. To better understand how a situation that appears to be based on individual decisions has systemic implications and reinforces oppression.

Materials Needed

Story "The Drawbridge" (p. 74)
Easel paper
Markers
Masking tape

Instructions

1. Read aloud the story "The Drawbridge."
2. Ask participants to rank the characters in descending order of responsibility for the death of the baroness (1 = most responsible; 6 = least responsible). This list should be developed based on one's own value system, not the values contemporary with the story.
3. Divide participants into groups of four to six persons. Have each person share her or his rankings. Then ask the group to develop a group consensus of rankings and a rationale for their decision. (All group members should be willing to stand by the final group decision if it is a true consensus.)
4. Ask each group to report on the final list, giving reasons for the choices. Record each list on easel paper.
5. Then share an alternative way of looking at each character as a symbol of some aspect of modern society:

Baron = white society.
Baroness = people of color and women.
Gateman = police force and military.
Boatman = institutions.
Friend = liberals.

This exercise was developed by Sgt. Charles Howard, Fort Lee, Virginia.

Lover = enticements (such as the Declaration of Independence, the U.S. Constitution, other U.S. ideals of freedom, justice, and equality).

6. Discuss whether this view of the characters in the story influences people to change their lists. Discuss the issues of power, blaming the victim, and action and inaction.

1. Give the groups ample time to develop and negotiate their final rankings.   **Note to Facilitator**
2. Depending on the results in each group, you may want to compare and contrast the assumptions made among groups.
3. Check to see whether the participants' responses change after they see the analogies to systemic dimensions. Ask: How often do we look at events as individual incidents outside the societal reality? How often do we blame the victims for attempting to gain something that rightfully belongs to them?

35 to 45 minutes   **Time**

The Drawbridge

As he left for a visit to his outlying districts, the jealous baron warned his pretty wife: "Do not leave the castle while I am gone, or I will punish you severely when I return!"

But as the hours passed, the young baroness grew lonely, and despite her husband's warning she decided to visit her lover, who lived in the countryside nearby.

The castle was situated on an island in a wide, fast-flowing river. A drawbridge linked the island to the mainland at the narrowest point in the river.

"Surely my husband will not return before dawn," she thought, and ordered her servants to lower the drawbridge and leave it down until she returned.

After spending several pleasant hours with her lover, the baroness returned to the drawbridge, only to find it blocked by a gateman wildly waving a long, cruel knife.

"Do not attempt to cross this bridge, Baroness, or I will have to kill you," he cried. "The baron ordered me to do so."

Fearing for her life, the baroness returned to her lover and asked him for help.

"Our relationship is only a romantic one," he said. "I will not help."

The baroness then sought out a boatman on the river, explained her plight to him, and asked him to take her across the river in his boat.

"I will do it, but only if you can pay my fee of five marks."

"But I have no money with me!" the baroness protested.

"That is too bad. No money, no ride," the boatman said flatly.

Her fear growing, the baroness ran crying to the home of a friend and after explaining her desperate situation, begged for enough money to pay the boatman his fee.

"If you had not disobeyed your husband, this would not have happened," the friend said. "I will give you no money."

With dawn approaching and her last resource exhausted, the baroness returned to the bridge in desperation, attempted to cross to the castle, and was slain by the gateman.

74

Exercise 13   Stereotypes and Racism: *Ethnic Notions*

1. To help participants see and question the stereotypes and images of African Americans that have shaped internalized dominance and white consciousness.
2. To break down these stereotypes and understand how they influence white people's thinking and perspective.

Ethnic Notions (video)
TV
VCR

1. Show the video *Ethnic Notions* (1 hour).
2. Ask participants to share their feelings about the film through "I learned . . ." or "I relearned . . ." statements.
3. Discuss other reactions to the film:
   a. What did you like or dislike about the video? Why?
   b. How familiar were the images?
   c. What do some of the media stereotypes about blacks tell us about how society regards or regarded them?
   d. What kind of effect do you think these media portrayals have on white Americans?
   e. What kind of effect do you think these media portrayals have on black Americans?
   f. What images of African Americans, Latinas and Latinos, Asian Americans, and Native Americans do you see in movies, television, and other cultural representations today? To what extent have they improved? To what extent have new stereotypes merely replaced the old ones? Which stereotypes endure to this day? How are whites portrayed?
   g. In what subtle ways do you feel that your own perceptions and ideas about racism have been influenced by media representations and stereotypes?

75

1. Many of the earlier representations shown in the video (e.g. Sambos, Pickaninnies, minstrel shows, etc.) are so shocking to modern sensibilities that some participants may see only the progress that has been made in the past one hundred years in defeating those stereotypes. It is important to recognize the ways in which certain aspects of those stereotypes (e.g., laziness or untrustworthiness, roles to serve and take care of white people) persist in the minds of many white people today.

2. When considering the new stereotypes that exist today, be sure to include the representations we see in music videos, movies, TV commercials, depictions of inner cities, and so on. While there are modern images of black people as doctors, lawyers, and other professionals, there are also persistent portrayals of black people as thugs, drug dealers, villains, gang members, basketball-obsessed, and so on.

3. In discussing current media portrayal, do not forget to look at exclusion. What are the most popular TV shows today? How many of them have black characters or characters of other racial groups? What kinds of roles are people of color playing?

4. It is important to extend the conversation to other racial groups. What are the images we have of Latinas and Latinos? Native Americans? Asian Americans? How are the stereotypes continually reinforced through the media?

Time

1 hour 30 minutes

Exercise 14   The Web of Institutional Racism

1. To identify various parts of an institution that support racism.   **Goals**
2. To look at practices, policies, and structures that support racism in an institution.
3. To look at institutional racism and all the ways in which structures, policies, practices, and behaviors reinforce the oppression of people of color and maintain a system of privilege for whites.

Easel paper   **Materials**
Markers   **Needed**
Masking tape

1. Ask participants to brainstorm the parts of an institution, using an   **Instructions** institution with which they are familiar.
2. Ask how each part interacts with the others. Does, and can, any part stand alone? Draw lines to indicate that each part interacts with others. Example:

The Web of Institutional Racism—University Setting

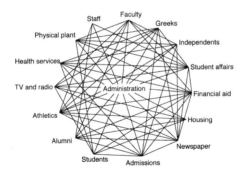

More arrows can be drawn to indicate further interaction of the parts.

Adapted from an exercise developed by Sally Timmel, *White on White: A Handbook for Groups Working against Racism*, p. 26.

77

3. Discuss practices, policies, and structures within the institutions.
   a. Who decides on policies?
   b. Who controls the policies?
   c. For whose needs are the policies, practices, and structures geared?
   d. What kind of controls or impact do people of color have on the system?

Note to Facilitator

1. It is important to discuss how institutions are created to meet people's needs and to understand the role that history plays in setting up the structures, systems, and processes that linger in an organization's culture. Explore how, and if, the institutions meet the needs they claim to meet. Again, it is vital to touch on the issues of power and control within the system. Who sets policies and practices? How does one gain access to power positions within the system?
2. It is crucial to deal with the inconsistencies. What is the institutional attitude, and what is the actual behavior? How do the policies and practices facilitate or inhibit actualizing the attitudes of the system?
3. It is essential for you to have a working knowledge of the system that the group is exploring.

Time

35 to 45 minutes

Exercise 15   The Effects of Institutional Racism on Native Americans

Goals

1. To expose participants to the effects of institutional racism on Native Americans.
2. To hear about these effects in a Native American's words.
3. To highlight basic inconsistencies in American heritage and behavior.

The Best of Buffy Sainte-Marie (CD or cassette) (selections "Now That the Buffalo's Gone," "My Country 'Tis of Thee—Your People Are Dying") CD or cassette player   **Materials Needed**

1. Play the two selections listed above.   **Instructions**
2. Ask the participants to share their reactions.
3. Discuss the following:
   a. The smallpox-blanket-for-land form of genocide.
   b. Manifest destiny—an excuse for genocide.
   c. Stereotypes of Native Americans (also known as Original Americans).
   d. Reservations, who has the power and control?
   e. The controversy over gambling casinos on Native American land.
   f. Native Americans and the legal battle over fishing rights and land.
4. Discuss the inconsistencies of "American heritage and culture" and the treatment of Native Americans.
5. Discuss how institutional racism camouflages the real actions of white Americans and disregards the contributions of people of color to American society.
6. Discuss media representations of Native Americans today. How are they presented? Are they presented at all? How many Native American movies, books, authors, musicians, actors, and so on, can you name?

These selections highlight issues of racism and genocide directed against Native Americans and expose participants to some of the   **Note to Facilitator** inconsistencies and hypocrisies in the present and the past. This exercise can also focus on the functioning of institutional racism in education as revealed by what is included in curricula and textbooks and what is left out. Discussions can also focus on the romanticization of Native American culture—and how we have forgotten that by law Native people in this country still cannot practice their religion and spiritual ways.

Time 30 to 45 minutes

80

Exercise 16   Debate

1. To have participants discuss an issue involving racism in a debate
   format.
2. To try to "stretch" participants' attitudes by encouraging them to look
   at both sides of an issue.

None

1. Choose an issue that you feel the group is interested in working on
   or needs to work on. Examples:
   a. Racism is the responsibility of white people.
   b. The power of white people in this group to combat racism.
   c. School vouchers—how they demonstrate white racism.
   d. Affirmative action: are whites being discriminated against?
   e. The Confederate flag—legitimate history or symbol of racism?
2. Form the group as follows: three judges, one timekeeper, a pro side,
   and a con side.
3. Give each side (pro and con) ten minutes to prepare arguments.
   Then divide the time as follows:

   3-minute opening statement (pro and con)
   2-minute break
   2-minute rebuttal (pro and con)
   5-minute open discussion
   1-minute summary (pro and con)

4. The judges then take five minutes to decide the winner of the debate.
   This decision is based on the way the arguments are presented.
   Share the decision with the group.

This exercise is optional. It should be used if time permits or the climate in the group makes
it seem appropriate.

Note to Facilitator	You may want to discuss how the participants felt taking the sides they were assigned, especially if the argument they supported was contrary to their beliefs.
Time	35 to 40 minutes

Exercise 17   Some Perspectives on Institutional Racism

Goals

1. To explore and clarify the effects of institutional racism on black people.
2. To be exposed to a black perspective on racism.
3. To examine further the inconsistencies between white society's ideology and its behavior.

Materials Needed

The Light Side: The Dark Side by Dick Gregory (CD or cassette)
CD or cassette player

Instructions

1. You may choose to play any or all of the following selections, depending on where the group is and the amount of time available or desirable. The following selections are recommended:
   a. "White Racist Institutions and Black Rioters." This selection gives an overview of white racism and white people's role and responsibility in it. It highlights inconsistencies in white American ideology as exemplified in the Declaration of Independence. This selection is indispensable to the goals of this stage.
   b. "American History." This selection shows that "American" history is really white history. It raises questions about who writes history books and the meaning of IQ tests.
   c. "Property Rights—Human Rights." Here Gregory discusses basic American values. The selection is helpful in revealing inconsistencies in priorities and attitudes prevalent in white American society.
2. Discuss reactions to the selections.

Note to
Facilitator

This exercise helps to clarify white people's responsibility for racism in America. The selections are meant to be confrontational. They are blunt and to the point, and the arguments are presented in such a way that they are hard for participants to refute. The selections are thus a powerful tool. They should be presented at a time when tension in the group is high.

Time

30 to 45 minutes

Exercise 18   **Exploring Institutional Racism:**
                    True Colors

To explore black–white relations and how they function vis-à-vis racism.   **Goals**

True Colors (video)   **Materials**
TV   **Needed**
VCR

1. Show the video *True Colors* (19 minutes).   **Instructions**
2. Ask the participants to share what they have seen and the assump-
   tions that they have made. Ask them to share also any feelings that
   they may have about either man and the situation.
3. Reactions, discussion. Questions raised should include the following:
   a. How did the "world" treat Glenn and John?
   b. How might this influence the way they see and interact with the
      world?
   c. Were you surprised at the two different "realities" Glenn and John
      experienced?
   d. To what do you attribute their different experiences? To what
      degree are they responsible for the advantages or disadvantages
      they received?
   e. Do you think the people Glenn and John dealt with consider
      themselves racist or prejudiced? Do you consider them racist or
      prejudiced?
   f. Discuss the role of power as it is displayed here.

25 minutes   **Time**

This film may be used alone, as a substitute for Exercise 4, or in addition to Exercise 4.

**Exercise 19   In-Depth Exploration of Institutional
                 Racism in Specific Institutions: Projects**

Goals

To help participants begin to identify for themselves the ways in which institutional racism functions.

**Materials
Needed**

Easel paper
Markers
Masking tape
"Inventory of Racism" (p. 87)

Instructions

1. Form groups of four to six persons.
2. Brainstorm a list of various institutions in U.S. society—business, educational, religious, community, and governmental.
3. Ask each group to choose one institution and, as a group project, examine how racism functions in it overtly and covertly. The "Inventory of Racism" will be helpful in this process.
4. Have the groups report. The time devoted to reporting depends on the format of the group—whether it is a long-term course or a short workshop. The project can be completed during a lunch period or a day or two later.

**Note to
Facilitator**

1. In this exercise participants begin to examine institutional racism on their own, as well as gain insight into the dynamics of racism.
2. If preferred, the groups may report at the conclusion of Exercise 20.

Time

1 hour (10 minutes to set up groups, 45 minutes for group discussions, 5 to 10 minutes' report time per group)

This exercise is optional for this stage. It should be used if time permits. Exercise 20 may be substituted for it.

Inventory of Racism

How to Look for Institutional Racism

Use this sheet to help identify areas in society where racism is evident. Consider some of the questions asked and note any examples you have witnessed that illustrate racism at work.

I. Employment
   - What percentage of workers are white? People of color? Men? Women? At what job levels and functions?
   - How are employees recruited?
   - Does the organization claim to be hiring from the "best and brightest colleges" (and then say they cannot afford to hire people of color because they are too much in demand)?
   - Does the organization recruit in local urban communities?
   - Is an employment agency used?
   - Is there a requirement that there be diversity in those holding high-level positions? Where are openings announced? Are openings at higher levels made known to present employees only? Are jobs advertised in the news media? In black community news media? In Hispanic/Latina/Latino news media? What is the current level of turnover? For whites? For people of color? Does the company use or have an employment center in neighborhoods of color? Is there an aggressive policy to recruit for diversity? Is there outreach to local communities of color to provide internships and opportunities for high school and college age individuals? To what extent are the sons and daughters of current and former organizational members hired and given preference?
   - Who does the interviewing? White individuals? Are people of color in decision-making positions? Are people of color involved only when there is a candidate of color? What training do HR professionals have in dealing with and understanding different peoples?

Adapted from Committee for One Society [Chicago], "Inventory of Racism: How to Look for Institutional Racism"; reproduced in Robert E. Terry, *For Whites Only* (Grand Rapids, Mich.: W. B. Eerdsmans, 1970), 101–4. Used by permission.

- What are the criteria for different jobs? Are they objectively and consistently used? Are they written down? Can they be written down? If not, why not?
- What are salaries at each job level? Are they uniform among employees at each level?
- How are people promoted within the company? Are there mechanisms set up to train for promotion? Is there a high-potential list? Are people of color seen as talented? Is promotion a formal process, or is it the result of social contacts? Comfort? Is promoting a person of color seen as a risk? Who rides together to work? Who eats lunch together? Do employees belong to social clubs outside of the company where company business gets done? What kind of special coaching and counseling is provided? Is there special counseling provided to help black employees face problems of competition with more aggressive and prejudiced white employees? Is there a company or union newsletter? Who writes it? Who does the artwork? Who prints it? Is information about training opportunities, and so on, communicated effectively to everyone?
- What kinds of facilities are there for workers? Recreational clubs? Teams? Where do they play? Where are company cookouts held? Who attends?
- Are tests used to screen job applicants? Are tests equitable for whites and people of color? What are the patterns of test scores for different groups? Who made up the tests? Have they been validated locally? Who administers tests? Who scores tests? Is there on-the-job training? For whom? How are people recruited for it? Who runs the training program? Are supervisors trained to value diversity and be sensitive to workers of color? What types of jobs are people trained for? Are jobs marginal or subject to elimination by automation?
- What types of employment benefits exist? Do all workers receive them? Is it company policy to acquaint all employees with health insurance programs, for example? Do executives receive stock options? Social club memberships?
- Is entry possible at all levels, or must everyone come up through the ranks?

II. In what capacity are vendors and suppliers of color used?
  - accounting?
  - banking (including mortgages and loans)?

- contractors?
- equipment?
- exterminators?
- food (cafeteria, etc) products?
- insurance?
- janitorial services?
- lawyers? doctors?
- maintenance (wax, bleach, etc.) supplies?
- office suppliers?
- repair services
- window washing?
- other?

III. Investments
- What property is owned? Is property rented?
- Who handles the portfolio? Through what bank or finance company?
- Who owns stock in the company? In what amounts? Who are the stockholders? Where do they live?
- What are the policies of the companies in which investments are made, in areas under consideration here? Employment?
- Are socially responsible investment practices used?
- Are policies of white suppliers in areas considered here?

IV. Advertising
- What agencies are used? What kind of contract? Size of account? Makeup of staff?
- Models employed? Images projected? Of product? Company? Society?
- Where is advertising done? What media are used? In what communities?
- Who does public relations work? Where is work done?
- How important is advertising? What proportion of business is invested there?
- At whom is advertising aimed?
- Are images of people of color portrayed? In white media outlets? In outlets of color?

V. Government
- Is federal government involved in business or program? Through what agency locally? How was it obtained? How is it used?
- Do institutions receive special considerations from local government?

- Who is the alderperson, congressional representative, and so on? Who represents the area institution is based in?
- Does the institution depend on a "good" relationship with public officials? Who?

VI. Board of Directors and Others
- Who is on the board of directors? What is the makeup of the officer group?
- What other boards do they sit on?
- To what social clubs do members belong? What voluntary associations?
- What do members get paid per meeting?
- Do members own a significant portion of stock in company?
- What other companies do members own stock in?
- How does one get on the board? How long does she or he sit on it?
- Is the board important in setting policy or only a rubber stamp?
- Where do members live?
- What are important social contracts and relationships with other influential people?

VII. Merchandising/Retail
- Percentages of credit accounts in white community? Communities of color?
- How are the credit ratings obtained? Who processes them?
- How does institution operate: Through the mail? Phone? Internet? Over the counter?
- Do people subscribe to receive the company's product? To receive information?
- Who is involved in granting credit?

VIII. Union (same questions apply to a union as to an institution in general)
- Does the institution hire union employees? Does the union have a diverse membership? Diverse leadership?
- Are new individuals recruited for the union?
- Are apprenticeships available? For whom?
- How does the union bank? Who runs the union?
- How does the union relate to local communities of color?
- Does the union have stewards of color? Officers of color?

IX. Community Support
- What contributions do companies and officers make to the community?
- Do employees get a living wage?
- Does the organization help employees get housing? Do they assure that there is no redlining with the realtors they use?
- Does the community have segregated neighborhoods?
- What kinds of support is there for local organizations such as the NAACP Legal Defense Fund, the United Negro College Fund, the Urban League, La Raza, the American Indian College Fund, United Way?
- How are money and power used to support issues crucial to communities of color?

X. Is there a company committee to develop and carry out a program for implementation of a nonracist policy?
- Company officers appointed to supervise a program?
- Regular examinations of compliance with policies?
- Education of all levels of management?
- Persons appointed to relate especially to black services and suppliers?

XI. What image is created by the company?
- Contents of bulletin boards?
- Menus in the cafeteria?
- Pictures on the walls?
- Decor?
- Music played while on "hold" on the phone?

Exercise 20   More Perspectives on Institutional Racism: *The Color of Fear*

Goals
1. To gain insight into how men of color experience the world.
2. To bring the voices of men of color into the group.
3. To share important dialogue among men of color with the group participants.

Materials Needed

The Color of Fear (video)
TV
VCR

Instructions
1. Play video *The Color of Fear* (90 minutes). Note: given the time frame, you may choose to show excerpts of the video or stop in the middle.
2. Ask participants what they learned from the video. What was surprising to them? What was not surprising?
3. Ask participants to identify and confront what was uncomfortable for them in the video. What specifically did they feel? (Anger? Guilt? Frustration? Shame? etc.)
4. How do they view dialogue such as the one engaged in by the men in the video?
5. What key messages are they taking out of the conversation that the men on the video had with one another. Have they ever had similar conversations across racial lines? If so, what did they learn? If not, what do they feel now, knowing that many men of color have perspectives and feelings similar to those expressed in the video?

Note to Facilitator
1. The video offers a provocative look at how some people of color experience the world. At times the tone is very confrontational and challenging. In many ways what is said can reinforce for whites why

This exercise is optional. It should be used if time permits.

they do not want to have a dialogue about race. It is therefore important to guide participants through their discomfort, acknowledging it but looking beyond it to identify why such discussions are important and how they can be productive.

2. Since this group of participants is not multiracial, the video also provides a means for letting them hear the voices of some people of color while maintaining the advantages (discussed elsewhere) of an all-white session.

2 hours (90-minute video, 30-minute discussion)   **Time**

Exercise 21   Reality Testing: The Racial Awareness Quiz

Goals   To explore assumptions about race that typically arise from traditional Eurocentric education and modern American media.

Materials   Racial Awareness Quiz (excerpt on p. 95), developed by the Center for
Needed   the Study of White American Culture
                     Racial Awareness Quiz Answer Guide (p. 97)
                     Pens and pencils

Instructions   1. Administer the Racial Awareness Quiz (excerpt).
                     2. Grade the tests as a group.
                     3. Discuss the participants' reactions to taking the test and their scores.
                        a. How they felt knowing or not knowing the answers.
                        b. What their scores indicate about institutional racism in education.
                        c. Who determines what is taught in schools and what is not, and the criteria on which such decisions are based.
                        d. Why they did not know the answers to certain questions and what they may have based their guesses on.

Note to   This exercise functions on two levels. First, it contains information—
Facilitator   often surprising to most white people—about the depth and history of racism in U.S. culture. Second, many people will not be able to answer the questions correctly. For many, this begins to open up the presence of institutional racism in education, since the information in the quiz is just as historically valid as what they were taught. Make sure that both of these points are clear when leading the group through the activity.

Time   1 hour (15 minutes to administer, 45 minutes to grade and discuss)

This exercise is optional. It should be used if time permits.

94

Racial Awareness Quiz (Excerpt)

1. In 1841, the people of Ireland sent a petition with 60,000 signatures to the Irish in America. What did the petition ask Irish Americans to do?

   a) Join the American Abolitionists in overthrowing the American system of slavery that held Africans and African Americans in bondage.
   b) Send money to aid the newly formed movement for Irish independence from English domination.
   c) Return to the land of their birth, no longer forsaking it for a new and untried country where they faced oppression as bad as any in the home country.
   d) Create a haven in the new world where more Irish might escape from the ravages of famine and start a new life in a surrounding that kept the glorious traditions of Irish culture forever alive.

2. The following quotation reflected the spirit and sentiment of the country toward race relations during which period of American history? "All distinctions on race or color have been forever abolished in the United States."

   a) 1867–1875
   b) 1900–1910
   c) 1930–1940
   d) 1955–1965

3. Which of the following wars was fought by an integrated army and navy on the American side?

   a) The Revolutionary War
   b) The Civil War
   c) The Spanish–American War
   d) World War I
   e) World War II

Reprinted with the permission of the Center for the Study of White American Culture. See Resource List for information on obtaining the full quiz and answer guide.

4. Which of the following racial/cultural groups is the most ethnically diverse?

   a) Asian Americans
   b) Black Americans
   c) Hispanic Americans
   d) Native Americans
   e) White Americans

5. In 1922 the United States Supreme Court denied Takao Ozawa, a Japanese immigrant, the right to become a U.S. citizen. What failing of Ozawa's before the law did the court use as a basis for its decision?

   a) He failed to be born White.
   b) He failed to learn English.
   c) He failed to show a willingness to assimilate to the mainstream American culture.
   d) He failed to forgo nationalist sentiments in support of Japan.
   e) He failed to obtain at least a high school education.

Racial Awareness Quiz Answer Guide

1. A

In the 1800s the Irish were proud there had been no slaves in Ireland for 700 years. So it was on this matter that the Irish of Ireland petitioned the Irish of America. The petition read, in part:

> Irishmen and Irishwomen! Treat the colored people as equals, as brethren. By your memories of Ireland, continue to love liberty— hate slavery—CLING BY THE ABOLITIONISTS—and in America you will do honor to the name of Ireland.

The petition was signed by Daniel O'Connell, the leading figure in the Irish movement to overthrow English domination. O'Connell, known for his work in Ireland as "the Liberator," said "God knows I speak for the saddest people the sun sees; but may my right hand forget its cunning, and my tongue cleave to the roof of my mouth, if to save Ireland, even Ireland, I forget the negro one single hour!"

The petition was received by the Abolitionists in America who publicized it through public meetings and the press. Irish Americans were unimpressed and proclaimed their consternation at being singled out, for they felt they did "not form a distinct class of the community, but consider ourselves in every respect as CITIZENS of this great and glorious republic—that we look upon every attempt to address us, otherwise than as CITIZENS, upon the subject of the abolition of slaver, or any subject whatsoever, as base and iniquitous, no matter from what quarter it may proceed."

Economic competition between Irish Americans and both free and enslaved African Americans was fierce. Furthermore, in the racial theories of native White Americans at the time, the Irish were not understood to be White. Some considered them to be Black. Thus Irish Americans, who remained Irish in their financial support of political freedom for Ireland, made a point of proclaiming their common citizenship with other White Americans on domestic issues. About the evils of slaver, they replied, "[T]he slaves of America partake of all the necessaries and comforts of life in abundance. They are visited by no periodical famines . . . and their slumbers are uninterrupted by the cries of their famishing children."

So complete was the rejection of this petition by Irish Americans that William Lloyd Garrison, the famous Abolitionist, wrote in July 1842 that "Even to this hour, not a single Irishman has come forward, either publicly or privately, to express his approval of the [petition], or to avow his determination to abide by its sentiments."

Source: Noel Ignatiev, *How the Irish Became White* (New York: Routledge, 1995).

2. A

The quotation was cited by Lerone Bennett Jr. in an article about the Reconstruction period of American history following the Civil War. Contrary to the beliefs of many White Americans, our history contains moments of racial enlightenment. But, as Bennett points out, these moments have been suppressed by the powerful forces of White supremacy. For a while it was not a foregone conclusion that White supremacy would prevail. It was only through the concentrated efforts of White supremacists, and the failure of White Americans favoring racial equality, that the nation sank into the abyss of Jim Crow oppression. It took a lifetime, from 1890 to 1960, for a more favorable mood to emerge. Even today the country still has not reached some of the high points of enlightenment achieved in that earlier era.

Source: Lerone Bennett, Jr. "The Second Time Around: Will History Repeat Itself and Rob Blacks of the Gains of the 1960s," *Ebony*, 50, no. 11 (1995): 86.

3. A

African Americans have fought in every war the United States has undertaken. For much of the country's history, troops have fought in segregated units. Segregation in the armed forces was officially ended by an Executive Order signed by President Truman in 1947 following the completion of World War II.

However, during the Revolutionary War over 5,000 African Americans and many hundred native Americans fought on the side of the United

States. Although there were some exceptions, most served in integrated units side by side with White Americans in both land and naval engagements.

Many African Americans distinguished themselves in combat, receiving the recognition of Congress and various civic celebrations and commemorations around the country. However, their story was later wiped from the face of American history—sometimes literally being removed from monuments—during the first part of the nineteenth century.

Characteristic of these times was James Forten, an African American who, when captured as part of a crew of an American warship and then offered his freedom, said, "No, I'm a prisoner for my country, and I'll not be a traitor to her." Forten was indeed imprisoned by the British on a prison ship where 10,000 other prisoners died during the war. He survived and became a successful and prominent businessman in Philadelphia, only to see his son later denied entry in the powerful trade unions that were then forcing Blacks from the free trades in favor of recent European immigrants. He died unable to provide his own family the freedom and opportunity he had so bravely fought for a few decades prior.

Source: Lerone Bennett Jr., *Before the Mayflower: A History of Black America* (New York: Penguin Books, 1993); Burke Davis, *Black Heroes of the American Revolution* (New York: Harcourt Brace & Company, 1976).

4. D

Native Americans comprise about 1% of the United States population but are the most ethnically diverse. One study found Native American tribes account for 50% of the identified ethnocultural groups in the country. In some ways Native American identity parallels that of White Americans who identify ethnically, but not racially. Tribal membership usually forms the basis of identification, with Native American or Indian identity being secondary.

There are 517 tribes recognized by the U.S. government, 365 recognized by individual states, and 52 self-identified groups. Despite their diversity, Native American cultures do share a common worldview with values that "are collectivistic and encompass a harmony of the individual with the tribe, the tribe with the land, and the land with the Great Spirit." This might be contrasted with European American values of individualism, competition, and aggression, nuclear family, and mastery over nature.

Source: Roger Herring, "Native American Indian Identity: A People of Many Peoples," in *Race, Ethnicity and Self: Identity in Multicultural Perspective*, edited by Elizabeth Pathy Salett and Diane R. Koslow (Washington, D.C.: NMCI Publications, 1994).

5. A

In every way he could, Takao Ozawa prepared himself to be an American citizen. He graduated high school in the United States and attended the University of California. He married a woman educated in the United States. In his home, he spoke only English so that his children would learn the language. He kept no ties with Japan, politically or socially. He worked for an American company and attended an American church. All in all, he fully identified as an American and made every effort to assimilate to the mainstream culture.

Through no fault of his own, Ozawa neglected to be born White and this was his undoing before the court. The U.S. Congress, in one of the first laws ever made in the new nation, had passed the Naturalization Act of 1790. This law clearly said only White people could become naturalized citizens of the United States. In 1922 the court ruled that Ozawa was not Caucasian and therefore ineligible under the 1790 law.

The 1922 ruling left some ambiguity. It seems anthropologists applied the term "Caucasian" to people from southern Asia as well as Europe. This included, in the parlance of the time, "Hindus." The following year, in *U.S. v. Bhagat Singh Thind*, the justices cleared up their oversight. Prior court cases, including *Ozawa*, had accepted the terms "White" and "Caucasian" as identical. In *Thind* the court ruled that scientific evidence showed a distant link between the Aryans of Europe and those of southern Asia, but the makers of the 1790 law had explicitly said "White." The scientific term, "Caucasian," was not even invented at that time. "White" was something understood by the common man, not scientists, and that common understanding did not include Asian Indians. In the wake of the *Thind* decision, naturalized citizens of Asian Indian origin had their citizenship revoked. The requirement that persons naturalized as citizens be White remained in effect until 1952.

Source: Ronald Takaki, *Strangers from a Different Shore: A History of Asian Americans* (Boston: Little, Brown, 1989).

Stage 3   **Dealing with Feelings**

Stage 3   Dealing with Feelings

In Stages 1 and 2 participants explored racism on an intellectual level by dealing with definitions of prejudice and racism. This approach may seem somewhat removed from participants' own lives and actions. Many feelings were experienced during those two stages, however, and those feelings form the basis for Stage 3. This stage focuses on more personal dimensions by exploring the feelings and reactions of each participant as a result of the materials presented in the first two stages. The exercises in Stage 3 are designed to

1. Support participants' sharing of personal feelings produced by the experiences of Stages 1 and 2.
2. Help them get in touch with their fears of and fantasies about people of color, as well as their reluctance to see their own action or inaction as racist.
3. Facilitate participants' efforts to sort through their feelings.
4. Help individuals become open about their feelings so that they can continue their exploration of racism on a more personal level in Stages 4 through 6.

In Stages 1 and 2 most participants were exposed to many new ideas and perspectives. After having been bombarded with sometimes shocking new information, they may have many questions and feelings. For some, these questions and reactions begin to cause inner conflicts. For years they have believed and thought one way; now they begin to see that what they have been taught or what they have believed may not be true or accurate (Columbus did not really *discover* America). Although some participants may have been aware that racism exists, its scope and depth may feel overwhelming. Conflicts and doubt arise. Their "truths" are being called into question.

Stage 3 is a crucial stage in the process of reeducating white people. It is not enough to deal with racism solely on a cognitive level. If participants are not touched personally—if their emotional base does not shift at this point—they are unlikely to change their attitudes and behaviors.

If participants understand racism only from an intellectual perspective, the impact on their attitudes is limited and rarely will produce any significant change in behavior. If, however, people are moved internally and involved emotionally in dealing with and understanding racism, there is a much greater likelihood that their behavior will change as well. They will have a personal investment—a stake—in the issue.

Stages 1 and 2 raised participants' consciousness about what white racism is and how it functions. Many people enter Stage 3 with a host of feelings, overwhelmed by the new data, confused about what is the "truth," and feeling helpless. Others may feel guilt or shame about being racist or being white and having internalized privilege. Participants may feel responsible for racism because they are white, and they may be angry about the way the system has treated people of color. They may feel shamed by what racism has done to people of color and to whites. In Stage 3 many of these feelings must be brought out and dealt with; otherwise they will begin to immobilize the participants and stifle growth in any positive direction. The exercises in Stage 3 help participants get in touch with their "here-and-now" feelings, deal with them, and move into a process of change and growth.

Stage 3 is also concerned with helping participants explore their unconscious feelings. Feelings at the unconscious level include fears and fantasies related to racism and people of color. A fundamental reason why racism continues is that whites are taught to fear people of color: "they" will take "our" jobs, "they" are violent, we are taught to not trust the stranger and not to get too close. These fears and fantasies may be a result of personal experiences but more often are based on the stereotypes and myths about people of color that our society and even family members perpetuate. Several of the activities in Stage 3 are designed to draw out the images, fantasies, and fears that white people carry and help participants sort through them.

The main objective of Stage 3, therefore, is to facilitate participants' discussion of their feelings, to help them to not only share those feelings but also to move through and integrate them so that they will be able to move into succeeding stages.

Method

Unlike Stages 1 and 2, which were primarily content oriented, Stage 3 is focused on process. The success of this stage, therefore, depends largely on the facilitator's "human relations" or facilitation skills—that is, your ability to help participants reveal their feelings, fears, and fantasies about racism and examine them. The supportive climate that has developed through Stages 1 and 2 provides a sense of commonality and trust. If individuals can rely on the support of the group, they will not feel alone with their feelings.

In this stage you again have a dual function—to be supportive of participants but also to be firm in presenting alternative perspectives. For example, someone in the group is telling about once having been robbed by a person who is Latino. Now the participant experiences fear of being robbed whenever she or he sees a Latino. To support that fear would only be supporting the person's racism. Your role may be to acknowledge that being robbed might well be a frightening experience but also to ask whether if the robber had been white, the person would be afraid of being robbed whenever she or he saw a white person?

It is necessary to probe why the person generalizes about race from one incident involving one individual and how one incident can thus support one's racism. In presenting an alternative perspective, you must also help participants explore the myths and attempt to break through some of their stereotypes. If participants express feelings of helplessness, you must offer the alternative of action—to assure them that there are positive steps that they can take. Feelings of helplessness, shame, and guilt immobilize people. You must manage to give support and at the same time further participants' exploration and integration of their feelings. To move the group through this stage successfully requires a good deal of skill.

The exercises for this stage have been developed as starting points that will probe the participants' deeper personal feelings. They are tools to facilitate further probing of attitudes.[1] The sorting-out process does not end with Stage 3, however. Participants should be encouraged to continue to work through their feelings and reactions during the remainder of the training program, outside the group, and after the program has ended.

Stage 3 is an indicator of how well the goals of Stages 1 and 2 have been met. If in Stage 3 participants display some confusion and appear to be caught up in their feelings, you know that you are probably getting through to them. The more their inner emotions are involved and explored, the greater the likelihood that they will be willing—even eager—to take action to address racism.

---

[1] An alternative approach for this stage is to use a combination of the unstructured T-group format with Exercise 25, "Fantasy."

Exercise 22   The Here-and-Now Wheel

Goals
1. To bring to the surface feelings that developed in Stages 1 and 2.
2. To determine participants' feeling levels.
3. To provide a structured mechanism for beginning to explore feelings.

Materials Needed

Paper

Pens and pencils

Instructions
1. Ask participants to draw a circle and divide it into quarters.
2. Ask them to write in each quadrant one feeling that they have *right now* as a result of the workshop.
3. Ask them to share their lists with the group or, alternatively, to share their lists in pairs or small groups.

Note to Facilitator
1. Your role is to help draw out participants' feelings and to gain support in the group for each individual's feeling level. The climate should be such that participants will offer their reactions and support to one another.
2. Have the participants try to clarify where their feelings are coming from—that is, identify the exercises or group experiences that produced the feelings.

Time

Varies, depending on the issues in the group

Exercise 23   Fears of Dealing with Racism

1. To have participants get in touch with fears centered on dealing with racism.
2. To help them express fears directly involving racism.
3. To help them explore myths and stereotypes connected with their fears.
4. To help them explore personal experiences connected with those fears.

Paper
Pens and pencils

1. Ask participants to list five fears that they have about dealing with their racism. When they have completed the list, ask them to write down five fears they have connected to racism—a stereotype, a personal experience, a myth, and so on.
2. Ask participants to share their five fears. Continue with the second list.

1. There are two parts to this exercise. The first deals with fears of confronting racism that may be operating in the group. It also looks at reasons why people may be holding in their feelings or preventing themselves from looking at their own behavior. Typical responses are "I fear discovering that I'm unalterably racist"; "I fear being misunderstood if I start to talk out loud in the group"; "I fear that perhaps I am more racist than I thought I was"; "I fear that I won't have the guts or caring to do something about it"; "I fear realizing my ignorance." All these fears indicate some kind of block in the group. You must help participants not only name their fears but also explore them. It may be helpful to ask questions, such as "What is the worst thing that could happen to you if your fear came true?" This activity allows participants to get in touch with the limits and boundaries of their fears.

107

2. The second part of the exercise is designed to help participants examine their internal fears connected with racism. These include attitudes built on personal experiences, as well as stereotypes and myths. It is important first to determine which category the fear is based on. If it is based on myths, for example, it may be helpful to discuss where the myths came from historically and how, as a result, racism has been deeply ingrained in all of us. If the fear developed out of personal experience, it is important to look at generalizing from one incident and see how such generalizing also perpetuates racism. The question should be asked, "Would a white person feel the same toward all other whites if there had been a similar experience with a white person?"
3. It is also important to discuss how we tend to fear what we do not know or understand. When we encounter people with a lifestyle or experience different from our own, we sometimes reject them out of ignorance or because their "difference" seems threatening. Often that is the source of our fears.
4. This exercise facilitates participants' in-depth examination of internal feelings centering on racism.

Time   Varies, depending on the issues in the group

Exercise 24   The Circle Break-in

1. To have participants get in touch with their feelings of power and powerlessness.
2. To have participants get in touch with their power as white people to exclude people of color.
3. To let participants experience how it feels to be excluded.
4. To explore individual feelings about this power as they relate to racism.

None

1. Ask the participants to form a circle.
2. Ask them to begin thinking about how they feel in that circle—being aware of who is in it and looking at and observing one another.
3. Ask one person to volunteer to step outside the circle.
4. Tell the person that the group has something that she or he wants. The person must find a way into the circle.
5. Tell the group members that they are to find ways to keep the person out.
6. While the outsider is trying to get in, you should process what is occurring.
7. After the outsider has reentered the group, ask for a second volunteer. Repeat this procedure until everyone has been outside the circle.
8. Process the exercise:
   a. How did participants feel outside the circle?
   b. How did they feel if they got in?
   c. What mechanisms or tactics did they use to get in?
   d. Why did they try to get in—that is, what did the group have that they wanted?
   e. How did they feel being a part of the circle while others were trying to get in?
   f. How can this exercise be related to racism?
   g. If they manage to get in, what made them feel a part of the group?

109

| **Note to** | This exercise helps participants explore their own feelings about |
| **Facilitator** | racism by drawing out their own power and helping them get in touch |

This exercise helps participants explore their own feelings about racism by drawing out their own power and helping them get in touch with it. The whole question of exclusion and fighting for one's rights can be considered. The exercise demonstrates how people may be supporting racism unintentionally without being actively racist.

Because this activity is physical, it is important to get everyone's agreement to participate. The other activities have been verbal; this moves the group into another realm and can be emotionally charged for some members of the group. Discuss the physical aspects of this exercise in addition to the emotional, intellectual, and psychological dimensions.

Time 45 minutes to 1 hour

Exercise 25   Fantasy

Goals

To have participants get in touch with their fears and fantasies relating to racism.

Materials Needed

"Fantasy: Bus Trip" (p. 113) or
"Whose Fantasy? or, Do I Know Reality When I See It?" (p. 114)

Instructions

1. Ask participants to find a place in the room and lie down in a comfortable position. Ask them to close their eyes and relax (you may want to do a relaxation exercise before beginning the fantasy).
2. Read aloud one of the fantasies. Ask the participants to imagine the scene and fill in the blanks in their minds. Tell them to note in their minds and bodies their reactions, feelings, and thoughts.
3. Ask them to share their journey with the group. Have each person finish before going on to the next person.
4. Discuss the meaning and implications of each person's experience.
5. Discuss other real-life situations in which participants have been made aware of their racial prejudices (e.g., riding in an elevator with a person of color).

Note to Facilitator

1. It is extremely important that participants do not compare their fantasies. Set ground rules before people share that indicate each group member's job is to listen and not to compare or evaluate each other's experiences. Ask each person to share as fully and openly as they can what came to mind through the fantasy. Each person's experience relates to her or his personal feelings and reactions. Participants who begin to compare or evaluate others' experiences and meanings should be stopped.
2. This exercise is a catalyst in the probing of white people's myths and stereotypes relating to people of color. It can be a very deep experience, touching on strong feelings and fears. Enough time should be allotted to allow all members of the group to be adequately processed.

Time   Varies, depending on the number in the group and the openness of the
                  participants

Fantasy: Bus Trip

You are taking a tour bus to New York City. It is your first trip to New York. The ride has been quite pleasurable . . . It is a warm summer evening . . . You feel . . .

You look around the bus and notice that all the passengers on the bus are white . . . You feel . . .

You are now driving through Harlem . . . You notice . . . You feel . . .

All of a sudden the bus stops. You feel . . .

The bus driver says that everyone must get out. The bus has broken down. You notice . . . You feel . . .

Complete the scene.

Whose Fantasy? or, Do I Know Reality When I See It?

You are driving home alone at night from a meeting. Traveling on a well-lit freeway through the center of a large metropolitan area, you see flashing lights ahead. You slow down and note that traffic is being directed off the freeway at a point where temporary repairs are being made. At the end of the exit is a detour sign directing you onto a shabby, ill-lit, dirty, seemingly deserted street.

It is a hot summer night. You have been driving with all the windows wide open. When you see the detour you . . .

As you proceed down the street, you see a group of people gathered ahead near a store on the corner. Some are standing in the street . . . As you slow down to avoid the people in the street, you see them turn to look at your car . . .

A man steps out of the group and moves toward your car with his hand raised . . . He has something in his hand that he is waving . . . He is also saying something . . . His expression is . . .

Then you notice that there seems to be someone lying on the sidewalk, in the center of the group . . . The people in the group have expressions on their faces that seem to be . . .

At the same time you see, three or four blocks away, flashing lights like those that directed you off the freeway . . . You feel . . . You drive . . .

Complete the scene.

114

Exercise 26   Personal Racial Experience

1. To have participants explicitly record their personal experiences and **Goals**
   actions concerning racism.
2. To prepare participants to move into Stage 4.

Inventory of Racial Experience (p. 117)   **Materials**
White Person's Questionnaire (p. 119)   **Needed**

1. Sometime before this session give out copies of the Inventory of **Instructions**
   Racial Experience.
2. Ask the participants to select from the twelve categories items that
   are most meaningful to them and to complete the inventory by
   describing a specific event or experience, including day, place, and
   circumstance, if possible, for the selected items.
3. Ask the participants to share a few of the incidents that are the most
   meaningful for them.
4. Discuss participants' reactions to completing the inventory.
5. Discuss patterns and similarities in individuals' responses to the
   inventory.
6. Administer the White Person's Questionnaire.
7. Discuss participants' responses and what they reveal about their personal relationships with people of color.

1. Try to focus on feelings connected with incidents instead of allow- **Note to**
   ing the discussion to become an intellectual one. Probe into why the **Facilitator**
   person remembered or chose a particular incident. Concentrate on
   asking how it affected her or him and what emotional impact it had.
2. You can also hand out a version of the inventory that is geared
   to African Americans so that participants can have an alternative
   perspective.
3. When reviewing participants' responses to the White Person's Questionnaire, be sure to ask *why*: why did they grow up with so few

people of color (or, if they had many friends of color, why was that?), why do they not number people of color among their closest friends now, and so on.

Time   Varies, depending on the issues in the group

Inventory of Racial Experience

For each of the twelve incidents listed, try to think of a specific event or experience—the day, place, and circumstance, if possible. As you review and describe each experience, bear in mind the following questions:

a)   When did it occur?
b)   What happened? What led up to the situation?
     What did you think, feel, and do?
c)   What are you doing now?
d)   What will you do?

Completing this inventory may take an hour or more. The detail is necessary, for adequate answers will depend on the uses to which the inventory is to be put.

1. Treating blacks and other people of color differently from whites.
2. Learning that whites created, maintained, and benefited from slavery.
3. Becoming aware of discrimination against people of color.
4. Feeling more fortunate than, superior to, or better than blacks and other people of color.
5. Trying consciously to be especially good, kind, helpful, or loving to blacks and other people of color.
6. Desiring to prove that you are really equal to or the same as blacks and other people of color.
7. Being angry at other whites for what they were doing to blacks and other people of color.
8. Admiring and wishing that you or whites were more like people of color in some specific way(s).
9. Feeling helpless as an individual to do anything truly useful in changing white racism.

Developed by Frederick C. Jefferson, University of Rochester.

10. Deciding to resist actively those social and/or political and/or economic forces that cause feelings of worthlessness in and subjugate people of color.
11. Wanting to get over feelings of guilt and shame about being subconsciously racist.
12. Becoming aware of the need for a spiritual center.

White Person's Questionnaire

Please answer all questions.

1. Reflections on your past:
   a. As a child, I [had/didn't have] friends who were people of color. If I did have friends who were people of color, we [did/didn't] play in each other's homes.
   b. My most significant childhood experience involving people of color was . . . ? What I learned from that experiences was . . . ?
   c. My most significant childhood experiences involving whites with respect to race was . . . ? What I learned from those experiences was . . . ?
   d. Other thoughts about my exposure to and experiences with people of color as a child . . .

2. Thinking about today:
   a. I [do/don't] have people of color who are friends. Which people of color social identity groups are present or absent from your group of friends?
   b. Were there people of color at the last two parties you had?
   c. Were there people of color at the last two parties you attended?
   d. Other thoughts about your life and its racial/color diversity today . . .

3. Imagine yourself in the future:
   a. Will people of color be at your funeral? If yes, name some.
   b. Do you feel more likely or less likely to develop strong friendships with people of color in the next 5 to 10 years? Why do you feel this way?
   c. Other thoughts about your future . . .

Developed by Frederick A. Miller, The Kaleel Jamison Consulting Group, Inc.

Stage 4   Cultural Differences: Exploring Cultural Racism

The participants have begun to own and address some of their feelings and fears related to racism in Stage 3. They continue their exploration of racism in Stage 4. This stage focuses on another level of racism—cultural racism. Here the participants will be introduced to activities designed to

1. Help them understand what cultural racism is.
2. Help them see white culture as a cultural framework and its impact in supporting institutional and individual racism.
3. Help them see connections between their own environment and actions that may support cultural racism.

So that participants will be ready to confront and examine their personal racism, they must first understand the roots of it. Much of white people's personal racism is developed and supported by cultural racism, that is, the ways in which white culture serves as an underpinning for our beliefs, values, and thoughts. Therefore, Stage 4 is a crucial stage in fully understanding one's individual racism. Stage 4 helps participants explore cultural racism—one group's (white people's) domination over another (people of color) in terms of values, norms, and standards. Stage 4 is concerned with exploring the dominant white cultural norms and their effect on our institutions and the disparate impact they have on people of color and whites.

The exercises in this stage examine the values that underlie the "English language," the customs of dress, the white cultural holidays, and the standards whites hold about what is "good" art and music, beauty, and intelligence. White culture in and of itself is not racist; however, when we act as if our norms, values, and approaches are the *only* ones—the *right* ones—white culture then leads to cultural racism. Cultural racism is also explored as the basis of many of the myths and stereotypes that white people accept about people of color, for example, myths about black sexuality and stereotypes about laziness or personal hygiene. Also examined is the notion of America as a "melting pot" and what that

121

expression really means—that all cultures must "melt" or assimilate or become white in their standards and values. It is extremely important that participants begin to realize that cultural racism does exist in the United States, in that everything and everyone is judged by white standards.

In this stage participants begin to realize how pervasive cultural racism is, in that it affects institutional values and thereby supports institutional racism, in addition to affecting and helping whites formulate personal values and thereby support their individual racism. The exercises in this stage demonstrate that this form of racism is integral to U.S. society. We can hardly escape from it in any aspect of our lives. The main point that Stage 4 makes is that the basic functioning of cultural racism is in the use of white standards to judge people of color, their behavior, and their lives. Participants begin to realize that the use of white standards (and the belief that these standards are really objective and fair) by individuals and by the system—as exemplified by college admissions offices, employment agencies, standardized tests, our definitions of what is "professional," what is "hard work"—to judge people of color is cultural racism. Fundamental to racism in general and cultural racism in particular is the notion that "our way is the right way." That we do not even see white culture as a cultural system makes this form of racism even more insidious. By understanding the underpinnings of white culture and how they are manifested, participants are one step further in their exploration and understanding of racism.

Part of this understanding develops when participants realize that people of color often have perspectives, styles, and cultures different from those of whites. A second part of this stage explores the fact that cultural differences exist. Gross injustices occur when whites assume that there are not differences between various peoples of color and white people—that is, when whites say, "People are people," or "When I see someone who's black, color is not an issue." Some of the exercises in Stage 2 are also helpful here. Helping participants understand the historical roots of blacks (Africans) and whites (Europeans) is a way to help them realize that there are clear differences between whites and people of color that must be noted and accepted.

Stage 4 also points out more inconsistencies between U.S. ideology and our behavior. U.S. ideology includes the belief that all people should have the right to life, liberty, and the pursuit of happiness. Pressure on one group of people to conform to the lifestyle and values of the dominant group interferes with that ideology. The present standards and norms, which were established by whites, are also inconsistent with that ideology and unwittingly are based in the perceptions of owner-ship—that whites believe we somehow own the system and deserve to create the standards by which others must abide. Stage 4 explores these inconsistencies as another component of the American dilemma.

Finally, Stage 4 helps participants draw some connections between the norms and values in their own environment and cultural racism. This insight prepares them for Stage 5, in which they will explore their individual racism more fully.

Method

Stage 4 presents a new set of dynamics for the facilitator. When you are working on the issue of cultural racism, you are drawing somewhat closer to the participants' own experiences, values, and attitudes. Individuals can become very defensive at this point. Looking at issues of culture, which are so much a part of the air we breathe, is a challenge; because white culture has been the norm, most whites are unconscious of its existence. In addition, a key value of white culture is its focus on individualism. Therefore, it may be more difficult for participants to see the patterns that we share as whites and that there really exists a cultural framework (even if each of us who are white do not ascribe fully to its tenets). On the other hand, by now there should be some acceptance of racism as a white problem, acknowledgment of the reality of racism, and willingness to learn more about the depth of racism. Moreover, by now the support system within the group should be well established, and the participants should be feeling a commitment to grow and learn together. You must process more closely personal behaviors and ideologies that seem to grow out of cultural racism. This feedback must be given immediately so that participants can become aware of the ways in which cultural racism affects their individual behavior.

In this stage the facilitation strives for an awareness of the functioning of cultural racism. Participants need to understand that racism is perpetuated when white standards are used to judge people of color and is built on the assumption that the cultures of people of color are no different from white culture. That is essentially the task in Stage 4. You must see that this task is accomplished, as well as prepare participants to look at their own behavior in Stage 5.

As in the earlier stages, you need to be supportive but also firm. Keep in mind some of the guidelines stated in the Method sections of the first three stages and follow them where appropriate in Stage 4 as well.

Exercise 27   Language: Cultural Racism Begins with Words

Goals

1. To help participants recognize that racism is deeply rooted in our system.
2. To help participants recognize that the English language supports racism.

Materials Needed

Dictionary (several copies, if possible)
Easel paper
Markers
Masking tape

Instructions

1. Ask a participant to look up the meaning of the word *red* in the dictionary and read it aloud to the group.
2. Write the definition on the easel paper.
3. Ask another person to look up the word *yellow* and read the definition aloud. Write the definition on the easel paper.
4. Do the same for the words *black, brown,* and *white.*
5. Compare and discuss the following:
   a. Definitions associated with the word *white* as compared to *yellow, red,* and *black,* all of which indicate racial colors.
   b. What the various definitions say to the participants about how the English language portrays the various colors.
   c. What the different definitions imply about the way the white culture sees people of color.
   d. Why English is spoken in schools. How that standard oppresses Spanish-speaking people, Native Americans, Asian Americans, and African Americans. How people with an accent are seen and perceived.

Note to Facilitator

1. Note that most of the words defining *white* have positive connotations. The definitions of *black, yellow, brown,* and *red,* which to many symbolize people of color, have many more negative connotations.

124

2. This exercise can lead to a discussion about why English is the dominant language taught in the schools. Discuss the following: What effect does this standard have on children of other cultures? Why is a black dialect called "nonstandard" English whereas a southern dialect is not? Why do many bilingual programs see knowledge of two languages as a deficit and not an asset? (It may be important to point out that the Treaty of Guadalupe Hildalgo (1848) guaranteed that in exchange for land, people of Mexican heritage could maintain their customs and their language. Also, Native Americans were forbidden to speak their native languages and in fact were sent away from their families to boarding schools and forbidden to speak their language or follow their customs or spiritual practices.)

3. Discuss how language demonstrates our view of the world, as well as our underlying values and assumptions.

4. This exercise begins to deal with the notion of the United States as a melting pot. What is the melting pot? How are people of other cultures supposed to fit into the melting pot, which tries to melt all peoples and shape them according to white standards, including white language? Why must all people conform, rather than have the freedom to live according to their own culture and standards? This exercise pinpoints these and other inconsistencies.

25 minutes   **Time**

Exercise 28   Language: Words Do Matter

Goals
1. To continue to explore the power of language in terms of cultural racism.
2. To continue to explore the ways in which the English language is used to support and perpetuate the racist system.

Materials Needed
Easel paper
Markers
Masking tape

Instructions
1. Ask participants to make lists of expressions and sayings that contain the word *white* (e.g., "white knight," "white as snow," "white-wash"). Then brainstorm lists of words and phrases that contain the word *black* (e.g., "black sheep," "blacklist," "black magic").
2. Compare and contrast the lists.
   a. How many items in the "white" list have positive connotations? How many have negative connotations?
   b. How many items in the "black" list have positive connotations? How many have negative connotations?
3. Discuss cultural values and standards.
   a. What are positive and negative in terms of colors?
   b. How do these values become translated and reflected onto people of color?
   c. Who sets the standards of what is considered "proper" English?
   d. Who has the power to decide what are the norms, for example, that English will be taught as the dominant language?
   e. How has cultural racism been institutionalized? Think of issues like "English Only" legislation and the approach in many schools with respect to ESL (English as a Second Language) programs.
4. Discuss language further. The article "Racist Use of the English Language" (see Resource List) is an important resource for this.
   a. What is the difference between the expressions "culturally deprived" and "culturally exploited"?

126

b. What is the difference between saying "Masters used their slaves" and "White captors raped the African women whom they held captive"?

c. Why do we say that fighting for rights in 1776 was a "revolution" but that fighting for rights in the 1960s and 1970s by African Americans and other people of color were "riots"?

d. How is the English language used to cover up the real issues of racism?

5. Discuss how the English language affects one's self-image.

a. What effect does language have on white children's self-image if they perceive that white represents all that is "good" and black all that is "bad"?

b. What is the effect on black children's self-image? Native Americans'? Others'?

Note to Facilitator

1. Participants may try to argue that words don't really matter or have any significance. It is vital to discuss the way in which words communicate attitudes and underlying perspectives of reality. Although people may not consciously be aware of how symbolism impacts our view of reality, it is a potent force. Finally, it is important to remind people that the old adage, "Sticks and stones will break my bones but words will never harm me," is indeed false and that the use of language has a powerful impact on each of us individually.

2. A second point to emphasize is how jokes—another form of language—perpetuate racism. By laughing at or telling a racist joke, we are supporting our own racism as well as others'. Make this point as clearly as possible. Even if we do not tell such jokes, if we remain silent when others tell them, we are colluding. (Some would argue that people will "know" by their silence that they do not agree. However, one white cultural norm is the right to remain silent, and therefore the other person has no indication whether you are in support or disagreement. We define this type of racism as the "collusion of silence.")

Time

25 minutes

Exercise 29   **Language: A Subtle Tool for Cultural Racism**

Goals

1. To help participants understand how the terms we use to describe each other affect our views of others and ourselves.
2. To educate participants to choose language that better reflects a multicultural and multiracial world.

Materials Needed

Easel paper
Markers

Instructions

1. List the following words on the poster paper:

- Negro
- Nigger
- Colored person
- Black
- Afro-American
- Caucasian
- African American
- Person of color/people of color
- Nigga
- Minority
- White

- Native American
- Indian
- Original American
- Oriental
- Asian
- Asian American
- European American
- Hispanic
- Latina/Latino
- Multiracial
- Color blind

2. Ask participants to respond to each term by listing their associations for each, the positives of the term (if any), the negatives of the term (if any), the appropriateness of using the term, and what the term says about the people to whom it refers.

3. Have participants consider the following questions:
   a) What, if any, is the difference between "colored person" and "person of color"?
   b) What, if any, is the difference between "nigger" and "nigga"?
   c) What is the difference between calling someone an "Indian," a "Native American," or an "Original American"?

d) Why do you think people may prefer to be called "Latina" or "Latino" rather than "Hispanic"?

e) Why do you think we use the term "black" to describe a group of people the majority of whom are shades of brown?

f) Why do you think we use the term "white" to describe a group of people the majority of whom are shades of pink or light tan?

g) To what extent do you feel that "you are what you say"?

4. Ask participants what language they think is most appropriate for talking about people of different racial identities.

Note to Facilitator

1. Participants may well conclude that we have no good language for a clear, unprejudiced discussion of race. This in itself is an important point to consider. Why is that the case and what does it tell us about language and about our concepts of black and white?

2. Be sure to move beyond straightforward definitions to capture the pejorative connotations attached to terms like *minority*—words that have taken on a "one-down" connotation and serve to reinforce oppression and racism. Discuss how the word *minority* reinforces for whites a belief that we are the majority (when in fact even in some cities in the United States we are becoming a numerical minority). How does the term *minority*, when used by whites, reinforce our perceptions of ownership and being one-up?

3. Encourage the group to talk about the power of names and name calling. In particular, the word *nigger* today wields a strong negative force, even though the word itself and variations of it (like *nigga*) are used commonly among some African Americans. From whence do words derive their power, and what license do blacks or whites have to use them?

4. Consider the historical context of the words considered here. What does society's movement over the past few decades from "Negro" to "colored" to "African American" tell us about race in the United States?

30 minutes

Time

Exercise 30   What Is White Culture?

Goals

1. To help participants see the aspects of white culture that may be invisible to them.
2. To help participants understand how we are affected by culture and how it underlies everything we say and do.

Materials Needed

Easel paper
Markers
Masking tape

Instructions

1. Divide participants into groups of four to six persons.
2. Give each group some easel paper, markers, and their own space in the room in which to work.
3. Ask the group to think of themselves as "anthropologists" and to brainstorm aspects of white culture. Specifically:
   • What do white people value?
   • What defines status in white culture?
   • What is white culture's concept of time?
   • How do whites communicate? Verbally? Nonverbally?
   • What celebrations/traditions/holidays do whites observe and how? What are our rites/rituals?
   • What are our aesthetics? Consider art, music/dance, religion/ faith, history, food, dress, games/play/fun, and definitions of beauty.
   • How would you describe the family/structure for white people? What are other relationships like?
   • How do white people show emotion?
   • List any other factors that help define white culture.
4. Regroup and review the items each team listed. Explore what is common across lists. Ask participants to discuss what they learned about white culture: What was it like to create the list? What did they notice about all the groups' lists?
5. As a group, discuss the ways in which these elements of white culture play out and how they underlie our words and actions. Discuss

both the positives and negatives participants see in white culture. Are they surprised to realize that white culture exists? Are there certain aspects of it that they find disagreeable?

Note to Facilitator

1. For many participants, white culture is as invisible as air: it is an essential, automatic part of our lives that is given little consideration or thought. It may therefore be difficult for people to list its qualities. Your instructions must be clear, and you may wish to include a few examples from the list that follows this exercise. Once the process begins and the initial hurdle is conquered, participants tend to start seeing many aspects of white culture and feeding off each other's responses.

2. Connecting white culture to our own assumptions and behavior requires another cognitive leap and again you must assist in this process. When discussing the "white way" of decision making, competitiveness, viewing self-worth, and so on, encourage participants to explore how this has informed their own lives and their own relationships. This is an eye-opening event for many participants; they learn that their actions are not just a function of their own individualism but are heavily influenced by a culture that they have previously assumed was the one right way.

3. At times, participants get confused about the difference between the values of white U.S. culture and the values of consumerism and capitalism—which are tied to white culture. It is important during this activity to be aware of the distance that participants put between themselves and this activity; often out of resistance and the fear of uncovering unpleasant self-truths, they will want to argue that there is no such thing. It is important for the groups to develop their lists. Usually there is 75 percent overlap of concepts and items, which illustrates that although we may argue that white culture does not exist, the elements are present in each of us. Not all whites have internalized every dimension of white culture; in fact, many of us have worked hard to not have these as our dominant frames of reference. In either case, they are a force and a standard that has an impact on our view of what is acceptable and right.

4. The results of this exercise will be used in Exercise 35, "Connecting with White Culture."

1 hour

Time

131

Some Aspects and Assumptions of White Culture in the United States

While different individuals might not practice or accept all of these traits, they are common characteristics of *most* U.S. white people *most* of the time.

Rugged Individualism
- Self-reliance
- Individual is primary unit
- Independence and autonomy highly valued and rewarded
- Individuals assumed to be in control of their environment—"You get what you deserve"

Competition
- Be #1
- Win at all costs
- Winner-loser dichotomy
Action Orientation
- Master and control nature
- Must always "do something" about a situation
- Aggressiveness and extroversion

Decision-Making
- Majority rules (when whites have power)
- Hierarchical

Communication
- "The King's English" rules
- Written tradition
- Avoid conflict, intimacy
- Don't show emotion
- Don't discuss personal life
- Be polite

Holidays
- Based on Christianity
- Based on white history and male leaders

History
- Based on northern European immigrants' experience in the United States
- Heavy focus on the British Empire
- Primacy of Western (Greek, Roman) and Judeo-Christian tradition

Justice
- Based on English common law
- Protect property and entitlements
- Intent counts

Protestant Work Ethic
- Hard work is the key to success
- Work before play
- "If you didn't meet your goals, you didn't work hard enough"

Emphasis on Scientific Method
- Objective, rational linear thinking
- Cause-and-effect relationships
- Quantitative emphasis

Status, Power and Authority
- Wealth = worth
- Ownership of goods, space, property
- Your job is who you are
- Respect authority

Time
- Adherence to rigid time schedules
- Time viewed as a commodity

Future Orientation
- Plan for future
- Delayed gratification
- Progress is always for the best
- "Tomorrow will be better"

Family Structure
- Nuclear family (father, mother, 2.3 children) is the ideal social unit
- Husband is breadwinner and head of household
- Wife is homemaker and subordinate to husband
- Children should have own rooms, be independent

Aesthetics
- Based on European culture
- Woman's beauty based on blonde, thin—"Barbie"

- Man's attractiveness based on economic status, power, intellect
- Steak and potatoes; "bland is best"

Religion
- Christianity is norm
- Anything other than Judeo-Christian tradition is foreign
- No tolerance for deviation from single-god concept

Exercise 31 Mini-Lecture: The Historical Roots of Cultural Racism

Goals   To help participants understand some of the historical roots of whites and blacks from which cultural racism developed.

Materials Needed   Chart, below, on easel paper

Instructions   1. Present the following chart to participants:

Cultural Components of Africa and England, 1550–1600

Cultural Component	Africa	England
Religion	Relativistic	Absolutist
	Pragmatic	Based on faith
	Magical	Moralistic
	Secular	Sacred
	Family-oriented	Privileged
Social Organization	Matrilineal	Patriarchal
	Polygamous	Monogamous
	Status based on type of work	Status based on lack of need to work
	"Man is what he does"	"Man is what he owns"
	Stratified, fluid	Stratified, rigid
	Family discipline	Institutional discipline
Economics/Property	Agrarian, artisan, commerce	Capitalist commerce
	Hunting, fishing	Artisan
	Collective property	Private property
Education	Informal (family, peers)	Formal (tutor, schools)
	Oral tradition	Written tradition
	Required interpersonal contact	Facilitated interpersonal separation

Adapted from Jones 1972:150.

134

Cultural Component	Africa	England
Time	Present, past fused Traditional (primitive) Little change over time	Past, future, no present Progress—positively evaluated change over time
Music	Rhythmic—body Songs secular	Tonal, melodic – mind Songs sacred
Worldview	Intuitive, superstitious Tolerant, open	Rational Intolerant, manipulative

2. Add to the chart or read the following excerpt:

Englishmen of the sixteenth century were very ethnocentric and hence were predisposed to dislike or judge negatively any group of people who were different from themselves. Ethnocentrism is not, of course, a peculiarly British phenomenon, as most culture groups tend to think that their way is best. But within the context of English-African contact, British ethnocentrism was particularly salient: the culture of Africans was not merely different, but at the opposite end of the continuum on practically every major cultural criterion. Most significantly, British ethnocentrism included the glorification of the color white and the vilification of the color black. With the omniscience of historical perspective we might ask if there were any other way the contact of white Englishmen with black Africans could have turned out. (Jones 1972, 149)

3. Discuss the following points:
   a. What are the implications of the English people's belief that the African culture was inferior to English culture in that it deviated from English norms?
   b. How is this ideology reflected in today's standards and beliefs?
   c. Which of the cultural differences shown in the chart have carried over into the dominant white American culture?
   d. What implications do these standards have for those whose culture differs?
   e. How are these standards reflected in
      (1) What is seen as beauty?
      (2) What is seen as intelligence, and what mechanisms are used to measure it?
      (3) What traditions are celebrated?

135

(4) What religion is most often practiced?

(5) What norms and values are generally accepted?

Note to
Facilitator
It is important for you to read *Prejudice and Racism* (Jones 1972, 149–68). This book is extremely helpful in developing the discussion of cultural differences.

It would also be useful to read *Lifting the White Veil* (Hitchcock 2002, 101–22) for a cogent discussion of white American culture.

Time
30 minutes

Exercise 32   IQ: The Fallacy of "Objective" Knowledge

1. To let participants experience firsthand the impact of cultural bias in standardized tests.   **Goals**
2. To explore "IQ" as a culturally biased construct.
3. To illustrate that all knowledge is rooted in specific cultural experiences and values.

Copies of "The IQ Test" (p. 139)   **Materials**
Pens and pencils   **Needed**

1. Hand out copies of "The IQ Test."   **Instructions**
2. Ask participants to answer all questions to the best of their ability.
3. Hand out the answer key and have each participant score her or his test.
4. Discuss with participants their reactions to taking the test and how they did.
5. Discuss IQ and other standardized tests and how it both nourishes and is nourished by cultural racism.
6. What effect do culturally biased tests and screening systems have? Consider areas such as college admissions, employment, housing, and other socioeconomic opportunities.

1. This exercise is designed to show the degree of cultural bias in "objective" tests and that what is considered "knowledge" is often bound to privilege people of certain experiences and education over others.   **Note to Facilitator**
2. It is important to focus on participants' feelings about taking the test. How did they feel when they answered a question wrong? When they answered one right? How did they feel in terms of relating to the material?
3. Discuss who develops standardized tests. What norms do the test makers accept as givens? How are the norms of these tests developed?

Which groups do standardized tests most support? Which groups do they hinder?

4. You may want to use an actual standardized test to demonstrate how cultural racism operates. Often participants do not believe that these "objective tests" are culturally racist. Specific examples are usually very convincing.

Time 45 minutes

The IQ Test

1. What is the name of the awards given out by the NAACP?
   a) The Dove Awards
   b) The Du Bois Awards
   c) The Image Awards
   d) The Nubian Awards
   e) The Progress Awards

2. Chitlins should be cooked at least how long before eating them?
   a) 1 hour
   b) 2 hours
   c) 8 hours
   d) 24 hours
   e) 1 week

3. Bantu, Donnie's, Black Thang, and Africa's Best are all brands of what?
   a) Hair care products
   b) Designer clothing
   c) Hip-hop record labels
   d) Greeting cards
   e) Frozen foods

4. When is Juneteenth?
   a) June 6
   b) June 13
   c) June 15
   d) June 17
   e) June 19

Match the author with the book:

5. Terry McMillan   a) *Devil with the Blue Dress*
6. James Baldwin   b) *In Search of Our Mothers' Gardens*
7. Nella Larsen   c) *Cane*
8. Jean Toomer   d) *Go Tell It On the Mountain*
9. Alice Walker   e) *Waiting to Exhale*
10. Walter Mosley   f) *Passing*

11. Which rapper was not a member of NWA?
    a) Eazy-E
    b) Ice Cube
    c) Dr. Dre
    d) MC Ren
    e) KRS-One

12. Who played Foxy Brown?
    a) Pam Grier
    b) Cicely Tyson
    c) Millie Jackson
    d) Sheila Ray
    e) Diahann Carroll

13. What instrument does jazz great Kenny Burrell play?
    a) Saxophone
    b) Piano
    c) Trumpet
    d) Guitar
    e) Drums

Match the person with the achievement:
14. Charles Drew   a) Won the Nobel Prize
15. Phillis Wheatly   b) Pioneered blood plasma and blood banks
16. Matthew Henson   c) First person to set foot on the North Pole
17. Benjamin Bannekar   d) First black American to publish a book of
                           poems
18. Jean Baptiste   e) Founded Chicago in 1772
19. Toni Morrison   f) Wrote the first almanac

20. Kwaanza lasts how long?
    a) 1 day
    b) 2 days
    c) 4 days
    d) 7 days
    e) 28 days

21. The term "props" refers to what?
    a) Parents
    b) Respect
    c) Cars
    d) Guns
    e) Marijuana cigarettes

22. Which illness is contracted exclusively by blacks?
    a) Sickle cell anemia
    b) Rickets
    c) Diverticulitis
    d) Lupus
    e) None of the above

Answer Key:

1. C	11. E	21. B
2. D	12. A	22. E
3. A	13. D	
4. E	14. B	
5. E	15. D	
6. D	16. C	
7. F	17. F	
8. C	18. E	
9. B	19. A	
10. A	20. D	

Exercise 33   *The Eye of the Storm*

1. To show participants how quickly a system of oppression can be activated behaviorally.
2. To illustrate how oppression affects everyone and divides diverse groups.
3. To encourage participants to consider the ways in which they act out prejudices and work to maintain their privileges everyday.

The Eye of the Storm (video)
TV
VCR

1. Show the video *The Eye of the Storm* (25 minutes). Offer background information on the video.
2. Break the group into smaller groups.
3. Have each group discuss their reactions to the video. Questions they may wish to consider (but should not limit themselves to) include
   a. In what ways did the teacher "institutionalize" oppression and privilege?
   b. What was most startling to you about changes in the children's behavior?
   c. What were some of the effects of privilege on those in the one-up group?
   d. What were some of the effects of oppression on those in the one-down group?
   e. What behavior supported the maintenance of the system?
   f. What are your feelings, thoughts, and reactions to the video?
   g. Identify some parallels with whites and people of color in U.S. culture. How do these issues play out daily in schools, companies, and other organizations?
4. Reconvene the large group and discuss some of the reactions and comments that emerged from the small groups.

Note to Facilitator

1. Be sure that participants note both the obvious and the subtle changes in the children's behavior and that they appreciate the ways in which the burden of oppression weighs heavily on those in the one-down group. Also encourage the group to use the example of the video as a template for viewing racism in U.S. society—and to go one step further to examine their own roles as oppressors who covet their privilege and act on it in myriad ways.

2. Call attention to the fact that the teacher had the power to set up the rules and the children who were one-up did not have to do anything to benefit from those rules (which is how most of white racism is perpetuated). Yet some of the children quickly adopted behaviors that protected their privilege and oppressed the other group. Note also that the children being oppressed could have challenged the rules and most did not (except Brian, who was then personally attacked). Such are the dynamics that perpetuate racism.

3. Share some background information. The children in the video were actually defined as a "slow" class. Later in the year when the children were tested in the Iowa Achievement Tests, many of them dramatically improved. They said that having been in both the one-up and one-down positions made them realize they could do better.

4. Often participants will be concerned about the impact of the experience on the children and wonder whether the parents were asked permission to allow their children to participate (they were not). The irony is that we often ask permission to teach about discrimination and yet do not need to ask permission when children experience the impact of oppression on a daily basis.

Time   1½ hours (25 minutes for video, 1 hour for discussion)

Stage 5   The Meaning of Whiteness: Individual Racism

Stage 5 brings us to one of the most critical points in this training program. Earlier stages helped participants understand the dynamics of racism as it operates in our institutions and culture. At this stage they take another vital step in their exploration of racism as they translate those dynamics into their personal beliefs, attitudes, and behavior. They do so through exercises in which they

1. Further explore white culture and develop a sense of positive identification with whiteness.
2. Examine what it means to be white in a white racist society.
3. Focus on the inconsistencies in their own attitudes and behavior.
4. Explore how they may be perpetuating racism.

Participants enter Stage 5 having explored cultural racism and cultural differences. Although by this point they may understand that people of color may have different cultural perspectives from their own, they may not yet see themselves as white or identify many of the values, beliefs, and assumptions that they hold as being based in white culture. This issue *must* be examined and explored with participants.

Stage 5 helps participants discover and own their whiteness. Included in this exploration are such issues as the following: What is white culture? Why do we, as white people, see ourselves as individuals rather than as part of the white culture and white "race"? What are the privileges of being white in the United States? How do people feel about their whiteness? How do we develop a positive sense of self as white people without it being based in a one-up consciousness?

The main objective in exploring the issue of whiteness is for participants to realize that being white is important in one's life and still plays a key role in U.S. society in how we are seen and what opportunities are afforded us. Whatever ethnic group one may belong to (Irish, Italian, German, French, English, Scottish, etc.), a determining factor of one's fate in the United States is whiteness. Being white makes us responsible for a system that is white and perpetuates racism. Participants must

147

also begin to understand in Stage 5 that because they are white and part of the racist system, they have certain invisible privileges. Stage 5 names those privileges. Once they have taken this step, participants are on their way to exploring their own racism.

The second phase of Stage 5 focuses specifically on the individual's racism. By exploring attitudes and behaviors for inconsistencies, participants can begin to get in touch with their own racism. Just as it was important for participants to see the inconsistencies between U.S. ideologies and behaviors in institutions and culture, they must also recognize their own inconsistencies. The exercises facilitate this process by having people explore their own attitudes, values, and beliefs. They examine their attitudes toward people of color and toward other whites, as well as ways in which conscious or unconscious attitudes may be perpetuating racism. The ways in which these attitudes develop are also explored.

To examine one's own behavior is challenging. Part of these data comes from participants' interactions in the group and what they have shared with each other. There they can look at how their behavior has been either consistent or inconsistent with their attitudes. Participants also look at whether their behavior is perpetuating racism: Are they doing anything that is actively racist? How may their interactions or inactions be perpetuating and supporting racism? Participants reach the point where they can begin to name some inconsistencies between their attitudes and behavior and recognize how their behavior may be perpetuating racism. It is at this point that they begin to realize a need for change and develop a commitment to change. This prepares them for Stage 6, in which they will develop action strategies to combat racism.

Method

Your role as the facilitator in Stage 5 does not differ greatly from that of the previous stages. You must confront participants wherever possible with their racism, both attitudinal and behavioral. You can draw as well on earlier stages to clarify and highlight participants' individual racism.

The first part of this stage centers on whiteness. One difficulty you may encounter is that participants may be somewhat at a loss about how to focus on their whiteness. They may understand that white people have a different culture from that of African Americans or Asian Americans, but they may not be in touch with what the white culture is. In other words, they may know what they are *not* but not what they *are*. You must draw on the work done in Stage 4 and apply what was developed with respect to the explication of white culture to the individual level.

One trap to be wary of is the reversion of some participants to their ethnic identities. Many people deny their whiteness by saying that their culture was derived only from their ethnic identity. Although clearly that is a part of one's cultural identity and heritage, in the United States we cannot ignore the role that racial identity has played. Many white immigrants have suffered discrimination, it is true, but because of their color, they and their families have ultimately been accepted. People of color, such as African Americans, Native Americans, Latinas and Latinos, and Asian Americans, on the other hand, have been discriminated against in the United States for hundreds of years, and many are still at the bottom of the socioeconomic ladder. Color also continues to be an issue in terms of our organizational and societal structures. It still plays a key role in one's ability to make it in the system and is a more prevalent factor than one's ethnic background or abilities. People can often hide their ethnic identities but not usually their racial identities. This reality must be examined in the group.

A second dynamic in the group may be the denial of responsibility for racism: "I'm not responsible for what my ancestors did." This attitude should be explored in terms of the privileges whites have because of the racist nature of the system and in terms of the fact that whites maintain, support, and perpetuate the system. Although they are not responsible for the historical aspects of racism, the historical dimensions are still playing out today—in the criminal justice system, the educational system, the health care system, and so on.

Another part of Stage 5 explores one's individual racism through one's attitudes and behaviors and tries to uncover inconsistencies in them. Your role here is to help participants honestly discuss their real values, assumptions, and attitudes as well as understand the reasons why an attitude or a behavior may be racist.

Finally, this stage may bring feelings of guilt to the surface again, perhaps deeper ones than those expressed in Stage 3. The role of the facilitator is crucial at this point. You must help participants to work through these feelings, not support people getting blocked from owning their whiteness, and get to a deeper understanding of themselves as white people in a white racist system. Guilt prevents people from moving forward and taking action. Participants must understand that their guilt alone benefits no one. It is important that they feel some internal conflict and responsibility, and these valid feelings should be supported. But the guilt needs to be transformed into a motivating force that will enable them to take constructive steps to combat racism instead of just feeling guilty about their role in it. This energy for action is vital for Stage 6.

Exercise 34   Adjective List: How I See Myself—My Whiteness

1. To help participants begin to explore their whiteness.
2. To explore seeing oneself as an individual rather than as part of a group.

Copies of Personal Checklist (p. 153)
Pens and pencils
Easel paper
Markers
Masking tape

1. Hand out copies of the Personal Checklist to participants.
2. Ask them to select from the list five words that they feel best describe themselves. If they feel that the appropriate words are not on the list, they may add words that they feel best describe them.
3. Ask several participants to share their words. Write the words on easel paper. Note how many people in the group had the same words on their lists.
4. Ask the participants to return to the Personal Checklist and select five words that describe them racially. Again, if they feel that the appropriate words are not there, have them add others.
5. Ask participants to share their lists, noting whether they changed any words on their second lists. Write the changed words on the easel paper. Note how many people in the group changed their lists and the kinds of changes they made.
6. Discuss the following:
   a. How did the participants feel while developing each list?
   b. Why did they change their lists?
   c. Why do people see themselves differently when referring to themselves as part of the white race?
   d. What does that say about white people, in that whites see themselves as individuals first?

1. You may want to discuss the individual-group issue—that is, that white people do not have to see ourselves as white or as members of a group. We have the luxury of seeing ourselves as individuals (which is one of the privileges of people in a one-up group), whereas people who are oppressed by the system can never forget who they are racially or their connection to their "groupness." The oppressed group is always more aware of their group identity than the dominant group is of theirs. In fact, one of the ways in which we keep oppression alive is not to see our groupness or our connection to other whites. By seeing ourselves only as individuals we have the privilege of doing nothing—and can distance ourselves from the actions of other whites that we might find offensive. (It may be interesting to see whether women in the group list words that indicate awareness of belonging to an oppressed group, as compared to the men's word lists. This dynamic can highlight the racial issue.) The important thing to stress here is that a member of an oppressed group needs the support of that group, whereas the oppressor does not need the group's support. Many people of color see themselves as part of a group first, whereas most white people see ourselves as individuals first.

2. Some people do not like such checklists because they feel pigeonholed and categorized. It is helpful to acknowledge that it is hard to define oneself in only five words and to emphasize that they are to pick words that best seem to identify themselves.

3. It is useful not to tell participants the goal of this exercise before beginning it. Participants' lists change when they realize that they will have to define themselves racially after they define themselves the first time. Therefore, to gain the full impact of this exercise, give each direction separately, as suggested.

4. You may want to add your own words, or develop a list of words, that you feel are appropriate to your own groups.

Time   30 minutes

Personal Checklist

1. Select five (5) words from the list below that best describe you

Accepted	Easy	Limited	Secure
Adaptive	Emotional	Misunderstood	Select
Afraid	Employed	Nice	Selective
African	Enraged	Normal	Separatist
Arrogant	Exploited	Oppressed	Sexual
Assaulted	Flexible	Oppressive	Sharp
Average	Free	Outraged	Sister
Bad	Friendly	Paternal	Smart
Beautiful	Good	Patient	Soft
Better	Happy	People	Soulful
Big	Helpless	Poor	Spiritual
Blamed	Hopeful	Powerful	Strong
Brave	Humble	Privileged	Supportive
Brother	Hungry	Proper	Tight
Brutal	Hurt	Protective	Together
Chosen	Independent	Protestant	Tokenized
Christian	Individual	Proud	Tracked
Confident	Inferior	Pure	True
Conservative	Insulted	Puzzled	Trustworthy
Controller	Intelligent	Religious	Undereducated
Creative	Invisible	Respected	Underemployed
Denied	Jewish	Rich	Understanding
Determined	Just	Right	Unemotional
Dignified	Knowledgeable	Ripped off	Uptight
Disappointed	Leader	Schizophrenic	Victimized
Dying	Liberal	Scientific	Worthy

2. Write any additional words if the above word list is not descriptive enough to reflect your true feelings:

Exercise 35   Connecting with White Culture

Goals

1. To help participants explore their white identities.
2. To connect the "theory" of a white culture with participants' personal lives and actions.

Materials Needed

Group results from Exercise 30, "What Is White Culture?"

Instructions

1. Divide participants into small groups.
2. Have them look over the lists the group produced in Exercise 30, identifying aspects of white culture.
3. Ask participants to pick two or three elements of white culture that they feel are important to them, or are deeply embedded in their lives or personalities, and consider the following:
   a. How is this aspect of white culture present in your life?
   b. How does it affect your interactions with other white people? With people of color?
   c. What are the advantages and disadvantages of this aspect of white culture?
4. Looking at the lists again, have participants identify which aspects of white culture serve them well and which are barriers to working and interacting with other whites and with people of color.
5. Ask participants to share their observations in small group discussions.
6. Reconvene the large group. Have participants report out on what each group discussed.

Note to Facilitator

1. It is important to stress that participants should find both the positives and the negatives associated with white culture. The goal is to see white culture as one culture among many, not one that is better or worse than any other.
2. When reconvening the large group, note that even though everyone in the room is white, there is still diversity among them as evidenced

154

by the different aspects of white culture that people relate to. Many will share similar aspects, but the group will also display a range of styles, behaviors, attitudes, and experiences.

3. It is crucial that participants do not deny what elements of white culture they have internalized. All people in the United States (both whites and people of color) have been influenced by the values, norms, and beliefs of white culture. If we act as though we are beyond that, we miss the powerful ways in which cultural racism affects our actions and interactions. Therefore, this activity is an important step in exploring the very underpinnings of how cultural assumptions have an impact on our institutions and ourselves as individuals.

4. You may also discuss how white cultural values, norms, beliefs, and behaviors affect organizations.

45 minutes   **Time**

Exercise 36   White Is Beautiful

Goals

1. To explore what it means to be white in America.
2. To explore participants' feelings about being white.
3. To facilitate participants' acceptance of elements of their white identity.

Materials Needed

Paper
Pens and pencils

Instructions

1. Ask participants to take ten minutes to respond to the statement "White is beautiful." Ask them to think about what it means to them personally.
2. Ask the participants to share their responses.
3. Discuss the following:
   a. How did the participants feel responding to "White is beautiful"?
   b. What difficulties did they encounter?
   c. What do their difficulties indicate about how we as white people see ourselves?
   d. What elements of white culture do they embrace?
   e. How do people feel about being part of that white culture?
   f. Do they resist identifying with white culture? Why?
   g. What aspects of white culture do they feel proud of?
   h. What is the cost to us as white people of not embracing elements of who we are?

Note to Facilitator

1. This exercise often brings to the surface feelings of shame and guilt about being white and having privilege. Having come to a greater understanding with respect to the reality and existence of white institutional and cultural racism, it is often challenging for whites to want to embrace and own elements of white culture. If participants see

Adapted from an exercise developed by Frederick R. Preston, University of Massachusetts.

only the negative aspects of white culture they cannot be true partners for change. It is important for participants not to see the world in all-or-nothing terms. Although white cultural norms support racism in our institutions and ourselves, they are just a cultural frame. Other aspects of white culture can be very positive—as long as we do not act as if ours is the only culture or the standard by which others are to be judged.

2. Participants may find it difficult to own the elements of white culture. Explore why it is difficult and help them delineate the elements of white culture as a group if they cannot do it individually.

3. This exercise can lead to further examination of the privileges of being white, as well as ways in which whites unconsciously perpetuate racism. You may want to refer back to McIntosh's list of elements of white culture and ask participants to create their own lists of the privileges they are afforded by being white.

4. You should also help the group identify positive aspects of being white. It is important for us to feel good about ourselves as white people. All too often whites deny our whiteness because we feel that being white is negative. If people have a negative concept of some aspect of their identity it is almost impossible to develop meaningful interactions and partnerships with people of color as partners for change.

30 minutes **Time**

Exercise 37   Exploring Attitudes: Self-Image

Goals

1. To explore how prejudices work to support one's self-image.
2. To explore further how individual racism operates in white attitudes.

Materials Needed

Story "After You, My Dear Alphonse," by Shirley Jackson (p. 160)
Paper
Pens and pencils

Instructions

1. Read the story "After You, My Dear Alphonse" to the group.
2. Ask participants to discuss the assumptions and prejudices displayed in Mrs. Wilson's attitudes and actions. What do her attitudes and assumptions do for her self-image?
3. Ask the participants to write down one of their negative attitudes, or prejudices, that is racist, for example, "I would never marry a black person" or "blacks are not as smart as whites."
4. Ask the participants to develop an advertisement designed to sell that prejudice to others. Include what owning that prejudice can do for you, what it can do for others, and so on.
5. Have participants share their prejudices and advertisements.
6. Discuss the following:
   a. What do our attitudes support in us?
   b. How do our attitudes foster certain perspectives of ourselves?
   c. Which of these attitudes do you hold?

Note to Facilitator

1. This exercise begins the second phase of Stage 5. Participants will begin to look at their own attitudes and behaviors and examine them for inconsistencies.
2. This exercise also helps participants begin thinking about the relationships of their attitudes to their self-images. If the participants can

Exercise developed by Carole Betsch.

158

understand the purpose for which they hold an attitude, they can perhaps change it.

3. Exercise 37 facilitates participants' exploration of assumptions. What assumptions do whites make about people of color? How do we act on those assumptions? How do those assumptions often center on or support racism?

4. Finally, this exercise helps participants understand paternalism as a form of racism. Why does Mrs. Wilson *need* to "help" Boyd? Discuss paternalistic racism as a form of racism in which white liberals treat people of color as needing our help and incapable of acting without us. Paternalistic racism causes whites to continue to feel one-up as we help "those poor unfortunate people with their problem" and to feel that we must be the ones to help even when it is not asked for or wanted. Paternalism also involves whites continuing to define people of color as poor and disadvantaged.

25 minutes **Time**

"After You, My Dear Alphonse"

By Shirley Jackson

Mrs. Wilson was just taking the gingerbread out of the oven when she heard Johnny outside talking to someone. "Johnny," she called, "you're late. Come in and get your lunch."

"Just a minute, Mother," Johnny said. "After you, my dear Alphonse."

"After *you*, my dear Alphonse," another voice said.

"No, after *you*, my dear Alphonse," Johnny said.

Mrs. Wilson opened the door. "Johnny," she said, "you come in this minute and get your lunch. You can play after you've eaten."

Johnny came in after her, slowly. "Mother," he said, "I brought Boyd home for lunch with me."

"Boyd?" Mrs. Wilson thought for a moment. "I don't believe I've met Boyd. Bring him in, dear, since you've invited him. Lunch is ready."

"Boyd!" Johnny yelled. "Hey, Boyd, come on in!"

"I'm coming. Just got to unload this stuff."

"Well, hurry, or my mother'll be sore."

"Johnny, that's not very polite to either your friend or your mother," Mrs. Wilson said. "Come sit down, Boyd."

As she turned to show Boyd where to sit, she saw he was a Negro boy, smaller than Johnny but about the same age. His arms were loaded with split kindling wood. "Where'll I put this stuff, Johnny?" he asked.

Mrs. Wilson turned to Johnny. "Johnny," she said, "What did you make Boyd do? What is that wood?"

"Dead Japanese," Johnny said mildly, "We stand them in the ground and run over them with tanks."

"How do you do, Mrs. Wilson?" Boyd said.

"How do you do, Boyd? You shouldn't let Johnny make you carry all that wood. Sit down now and eat lunch, both of you."

"Why shouldn't he carry the wood, Mother? It's his wood. We got it at his place."

"Johnny," Mrs. Wilson said, "go on and eat your lunch."

"Sure," Johnny said. He held out the dish of scrambled eggs to Boyd. "After you, my dear Alphonse," Johnny said.

From Shirley Jackson, *The Lottery and Other Stories* (New York: Noonday Press, 1991).

"After *you*, my dear Alphonse," Boyd said.

"After *you*, my dear Alphonse," Johnny said. They began to giggle.

"Are you hungry, Boyd?" Mrs. Wilson asked.

"Yes, Mrs. Wilson."

"Well, don't let Johnny stop you. He always fusses about eating so you just see that you get a good lunch. There's plenty of food here for you to have all you want."

"Thank you, Mrs. Wilson."

"Come on, Boyd," Johnny said. He pushed half the scrambled eggs onto Boyd's plate. Boyd watched while Mrs. Wilson put a dish of stewed tomatoes beside his plate.

"Boyd don't eat tomatoes, do you, Boyd?" Johnny said.

"Doesn't eat tomatoes, Johnny. And just because you don't like them, don't say that about Boyd. Boyd will eat *anything*."

"Bet he won't," Johnny said, attacking his scrambled eggs.

"Boyd wants to grow up and be a big strong man so he can work hard," Mrs. Wilson said. "I'll bet Boyd's father eats stewed tomatoes."

"My father eats anything he wants to," Boyd said.

"So does mine," Johnny said. "Sometimes he doesn't eat hardly anything. He's a little guy, though. Wouldn't hurt a flea."

"Mine's a little guy, too," Boyd said.

"I'll bet he's strong, though," Mrs. Wilson said. She hesitated. "Does he . . . work?"

"Sure," Johnny said. "Boyd's father works in a factory."

"There, you see?" Mrs. Wilson said. "And he certainly has to be strong to do that—all that lifting and carrying at a factory."

"Boyd's father doesn't have to," Johnny said. "He's a foreman."

Mrs. Wilson felt defeated. "What does your mother do, Boyd?"

"My mother?" Boyd was surprised. "She takes care of us kids."

"Oh. She doesn't work, then?"

"Why should she?" Johnny said through a mouthful of eggs. "You don't work."

"You really don't want any stewed tomatoes, Boyd?"

"No, thank you, Mrs. Wilson," Boyd said.

"No, thank you, Mrs. Wilson, no, thank you, Mrs. Wilson, no, thank you, Mrs. Wilson," Johnny said. "Boyd's sister's going to work, though. She's going to be a teacher."

"That's a very fine attitude for her to have, Boyd," Mrs. Wilson restrained an impulse to pat Boyd on the head. "I imagine you're all very proud of her?"

"I guess so," Boyd said.

161

"What about all your other brothers and sisters? I guess all of you want to make just as much of yourselves as you can."

"There's only me and Jean," Boyd said. "I don't know yet what I want to be when I grow up."

"We're going to be tank drivers, Boyd and me," Johnny said.

"Zoom." Mrs. Wilson caught Boyd's glass of milk as Johnny's napkin ring suddenly transformed into a tank, plowed heavily across the table.

"Look, Johnny," Boyd said. "Here's a foxhole. I'm shooting at you."

Mrs. Wilson, with the speed born of long experience, took the gingerbread off the shelf and placed it carefully between the tank and the foxhole.

"Now eat as much as you want to, Boyd," she said. "I want to see you get filled up."

"Boyd eats a lot, but not as much as I do," Johnny said. "I'm bigger than he is."

"You're not much bigger," Boyd said. "I can beat you running."

Mrs. Wilson took a deep breath. "Boyd, Johnny has some suits that are a little too small for him, and a winter coat. It's not new, of course, but there's lots of wear in it still. And I have a few dresses that your mother or sister could probably use. Your mother can make them over into lots of things for all of you, and I'd be very happy to give them to you. Suppose before you leave I make up a big bundle and then you and Johnny can take it over to your mother right away . . ." Her voice trailed off as she saw Boyd's puzzled expression.

"But I have plenty of clothes, thank you," he said. "And I don't think my mother knows how to sew very well, and anyway I guess we buy about everything we need. Thank you very much, though."

"We don't have time to carry that old stuff around, Mother," Johnny said. "We got to play tanks with the kids today."

Mrs. Wilson lifted the plate of gingerbread off the table as Boyd was about to take another piece. "There are many little boys like you, Boyd, who would be very grateful for the clothes someone was kind enough to give them."

"Boyd will take them if you want him to, Mother," Johnny said.

"I didn't mean to make you mad, Mrs. Wilson," Boyd said.

"Don't think I'm angry, Boyd. I'm just disappointed in you, that's all. Now let's not say anything more about it."

She began clearing the plates off the table, and Johnny took Boyd's hand and pulled him to the door. "Bye, Mother," Johnny said. Boyd stood for a minute, staring at Mrs. Wilson's back.

162

"After you, my dear Alphonse," Johnny said, holding the door open.
"Is your mother still mad?" Mrs. Wilson heard Boyd ask in a low voice.
"I don't know," Johnny said. "She's screwy sometimes."
"So's mine," Boyd said. He hesitated. "After *you*, my dear Alphonse."

Exercise 38   Clarifying Attitudes

Goals
1. To help participants get in touch with their values centering on racism.
2. To help participants identify their attitudes and behaviors in a racial situation.
3. To highlight inaction as a perpetuation of racism.

Materials Needed
Values Clarification Exercise (p. 166)
Paper
Pens and pencils

Instructions
1. Read the Values Clarification Exercise to the group.
2. Ask the participants to rank from 1 to 6 according to their values who was "most wrong" (1) to "most right" (6) in the exercise.
3. Divide the group into groups of four to six persons. Have individuals share their lists and then have the group develop a list that all of them agree on.
4. Have the small groups share their lists with the large group. Have them also share their reasons for their choices.
5. Discuss the differences in the lists and the values represented.
6. Ask participants what they would have done in the situation and whether they have been in a similar situation.

Note to Facilitator
1. This exercise can be changed to make it appropriate for the specific situation. It is essential, however, for the values of the six people in the exercise to be somewhat close to those represented in the Values Clarification Exercise. The characters and the values they represent in this exercise are
   • Bill—goes through the system to achieve his goals.
   • Sylvia—holds the power and gives the okay but then buckles to resistance; is responsible for the situation in that she could have averted it if she had used the power she had.

164

- Jerry—states his racist opinion while trying to diffuse it as a joke.
- Ellen—inactive; although she could use her power to speak up and support the African American employees, she instead colludes in silence, ultimately supporting the racism of other whites.
- Mark—blatantly and destructively racist.
- Alicia—violent in retaliation, out of frustration, anger, and rage.

2. This exercise dramatizes the issues of power, violence, and inaction. It helps clarify and assess participants' real attitudes, that is, whether they reflect an understanding of racism. The processing of this exercise can confront participants with inconsistencies in their expressed attitudes and their actual choices.

3. Share with the group the information about the characters given above after the report of each group. Does this information produce any change in the participants' original lists?

35 minutes   **Time**

Values Clarification Exercise

The setting is a division of a large U.S. corporation.

Bill, a new African American employee, is starting a Black Employee Network Group at the company. He begins by asking Sylvia, a white woman who is the division director, for permission to organize the group, including advertising on company bulletin boards, putting notices in the company newsletter, and meeting in a large conference room during lunch hours and after work. Sylvia approves the request. Fifteen employees in a division of 140 sign up for the group.

As word about the support group begins to spread, several employees make comments. Jerry jokes with others at lunch that they should form a "White Employee Network Group." Ellen, seated at the table, thinks this is in poor taste and understands the need for a black network group but says nothing. Finally one white employee, Mark, openly complains to the director. He says that having such a group is divisive and injects race into the company. He accuses the employees of "playing the race card" and lobbying for "special privileges." He is especially bothered that the group is sanctioned by the company and is allowed to meet on the premises during working hours—clearly preferential treatment based on race, he argues.

Sylvia is uncomfortable with the brewing controversy and reverses her initial decision, telling Bill that the company will not endorse such a group and that they cannot advertise or meet in the building. She says it would be unfair to others in the organization for the company to sponsor a group designed only for certain employees.

When Bill relays this information to the group, Alicia is incensed. She takes a marker and writes the word RACIST on Sylvia's door, an act that will ultimately get her dismissed from the company.

Exercise 39   Exploration of Racist Attitudes

1. To help participants become aware of racist attitudes they presently accept or previously accepted.
2. To explore the myths behind some of these attitudes.
3. To help participants understand how and why these attitudes are racist.

Materials Needed

Copies of "Thirty Statements" (p. 169)
Pens and pencils

Instructions

1. Have the participants fill out the "Thirty Statements" sheet, putting an X before those statements that represent their current attitudes and an O before those statements that represent previously held attitudes. They are to leave blank those attitudes they have never held.
2. Have participants share their responses, indicating why they changed previously held attitudes or why they maintain present attitudes and how they feel about them. Your role, and the role of the group, is to clarify the racism in each of the statements.
3. Discuss participants' reactions.
   a. Do they understand why a given statement is racist?
   b. On what myths are the attitudes based?

Note to Facilitator

1. This exercise is long and can become somewhat tedious if each statement is discussed. It may be useful to ask participants to choose those statements that are of particular importance to them now, or those statements that shaped their upbringing in powerful ways.
2. This exercise often seems to clarify much of the participants' confusion. They have heard and believed many of the attitudes expressed in the statements, and the explanations help them adjust their perspectives and develop a better understanding of the racism in the attitudes.

Adapted from an exercise developed by James M. Edler.

3. Obviously, you must also be aware of the subtler issues of racism in the statements.

Time   1 hour

Thirty Statements

_____ 1. I am not racist.

_____ 2. I don't understand what you people are saying or what you want.

_____ 3. On the whole, the educated, the upper classes, the emotionally mature, and the deeply religious are much less racist.

_____ 4. Other ethnic groups have had to struggle. Why is this so different?

_____ 5. Angry people of color make me feel so helpless.

_____ 6. Racism exists only where people of color exist.

_____ 7. No matter what I say, it doesn't satisfy them (people of color).

_____ 8. If you could just get people feeling good about themselves, there would be much less racism.

_____ 9. Blacks and Latinos are more violent than whites.

_____ 10. I'm not a racist, but when it comes right down to it, I wouldn't marry a black person.

_____ 11. I should not be held responsible for the actions of my ancestors.

_____ 12. I'm with them (people of color) up to the point where they (want to) break the law.

_____ 13. These days whenever a person of color sneezes, thirty-seven white people rush up to wipe her or his nose.

_____ 14. People of color must be present in order for whites to address issues of racism.

_____ 15. How can I address racism without being anti-white?

_____ 16. I do not personally have responsibility for the policies of racist institutions.

_____ 17. People of color are just as racist as whites.

_____ 18. White people should not have to integrate if they don't want to.

_____ 19. Love cannot be legislated.

Developed by Gerald Weinstein, Leonard Smith, and James Edler, University of Massachusetts.

169

_____ 20. Immigrants need to learn to speak English—after all, my parents came here and had to learn English to be successful.

_____ 21. Every person should be judged solely on her or his accomplishments, regardless of race.

_____ 22. Because of the civil rights legislation of the past forty years, blacks have greater responsibility to exploit the opportunities made available to them.

_____ 23. We (whites) should get a little more appreciation for what we're doing to help.

_____ 24. I've gotten to know some black people so well that I just don't see them as black anymore.

_____ 25. Some of my best friends are black (or Latino, or Asian American, or Native American . . .).

_____ 26. They don't want us to deal with their problems.

_____ 27. Every time I express my opinion to a person of color, I feel put down.

_____ 28. On the basis of statistics, it is true that there is a higher crime rate in black and Latino neighborhoods.

_____ 29. People of color are more aware of their feelings.

_____ 30. In many situations, people of color are paranoid and oversensitive. They read more into the situation than is really there.

Clarification of the Thirty Statements

Below are descriptions of the racist assumptions in some of the statements.

1. Denies responsibility for perpetuating and benefiting from a racist system and ignores the many ways in which one's attitudes and actions display and contribute to racism.
2. Feigns ignorance of legitimate demands made by people of color for the basic ideals of all people—justice, equity, pluralism, human-heartedness, and so on.
3. Assumes that racism is an individual matter rather than one of all whites who partake of the benefits of a white racist society.
4. Shows a deep ignorance of the special deprivations suffered by black people because of whites.
5. A "cop-out" from white responsibility for dealing with white racism. The statement blames people of color for making whites feel helpless—a special example of "blaming the victim."
8. Denies the fact of institutional racism and every white person's responsibility to combat it.
10. A contradiction—self-evident.
11. Avoids whites' current responsibility to deal with current racism. We are all guilty by failing to take action and by partaking of the benefits of a white racist society.
13. Denies or minimizes how little things have changed for people of color in basic ways.
15. Assumes that there can be no true pluralism.
18–19. Denies legitimate human rights by treating the problem as one of individuals' feelings.
20. Mistakenly equates the situation faced by white immigrants to the racist systems faced by people of color and assumes the same opportunities exist for each group.
21. This is a statement for equality rather than for equity and can perpetuate racism by systematically ignoring the larger investment required by blacks to attain the same accomplishments because of white racism.

171

23. Should a child beater be appreciated when she or he beats a child less hard? *Justice* is appreciated.
24. Denies blackness.
25. Insidious patronizing attitude—suggests a superior position of the white person.
26. Injustices, and so on, are not "their" problems but whites' problems.
28. Blaming the victim does not adequately account for what white institutions have done to produce these results.

Exercise 40   Assessing One's Understanding of Individual Racism

1. To assess participants' understanding of whiteness and racism.
2. To help participants see inconsistencies in attitudes that are racist.
3. To further participants' understanding and owning of whiteness.

Copies of "A Vision of Equality" (p. 175)
Pens and pencils

1. Ask participants to read "A Vision of Equality."
2. Ask individuals to underline the assumptions (implicit and explicit) with which they agree.
3. Ask participants to share their underlined statements.
4. Discuss the following:
   a. What assumptions are being made?
   b. Why do you agree with them?
5. Issues to be covered include
   a. The writer's belief in the myths
      My parents could make it.
      The U.S.A. is the land of opportunity.
      I've had to work hard (belief that hard work = success).
      The melting pot theory.
   b. The writer's denial of her or his whiteness
      Wanting to be seen as different from other whites.
      Not wanting to be stereotyped.
      Anger at the system for being labeled.
   c. The writer's inconsistencies (not wanting people to divide themselves and then discussing "black and white").
   d. The writer's lack of awareness and understanding of institutional racism; reverse racism; wanting a society based on "quality and individuality."
   e. The writer's language, including the term "minorities," and what it reveals about attitude.

Note to **Facilitator**	1. This rebuttal is loaded with racist assumptions. Many participants still find themselves struggling with their whiteness. This exercise helps them understand how their whiteness has served to their advantage in accruing benefits of the system. By denying one's whiteness and the importance of color in getting ahead, one is also denying her or his racism. 2. It is also crucial to note once again the reliance on and belief in the myths. Highlight the discrepancies between ideology and behavior.
Time	45 minutes

A Vision of Equality

Underline the assumptions (implicit and explicit) with which you agree.

I'm a person too. I'm tired of being told I'm responsible for the sins of my ancestors. Why, my family didn't arrive in this country until after World War II. They were oppressed in Europe and came to the United States seeking opportunity and a better life.

My parents worked hard. They came to this country without knowing a word of English and had to learn the language to be successful. They struggled and made it on their own. I've had to work hard too. No one gave me a handout to get through college. Since my family couldn't afford to send me, I supported myself. Now, after all my hard work, I turn around and a less qualified minority is getting the job I deserve.

I agree that minorities have been discriminated against. But now we're discriminating in reverse. I feel that I'm being lumped together with all other whites and stereotyped. My humanity is being denied. My individuality is just as important to me as it is to minorities. I'm all for equality, but let's make it both ways.

It disturbs me to see people dividing themselves. We've got to learn to get along with each other, and the only way we can do that is by treating each other as individuals, not as black or white. People are people, and once we realize that, we can achieve a society which rewards quality and individuality.

Developed in collaboration with Glenn S. Phillips, University of Oklahoma.

Exercise 41 Discovering Inconsistencies between Attitudes and Behavior

Goals
1. To identify one's values and attitudes centering on racism.
2. To explore one's behavior based on those values.
3. To discover inconsistencies between values and behavior.

Materials Needed

Paper

Pens and pencils

Instructions
1. Ask participants to take a piece of paper and divide it into four columns, headed as follows:

I Values/Attitudes	II Actions I Have Taken	III Consistency	IV

2. Ask participants to think of one positive anti-racist attitude or value they hold, for example, "Whites are responsible for racism." List this attitude in Column I.
3. Ask participants to list in Column II specific actions they have taken on that attitude: "I have worked to reeducate my friend about her racism," or "I have pushed for more people of color in city government to ensure their needs are addressed." If they have no corresponding actions for the value/attitude in Column I, they are to leave Column II blank.
4. Tell the participants that if they have taken actions that seem consistent with that attitude, they are to check Column III. If not, they are to leave Column III blank.
5. Participants are to leave Column IV blank for now. It will be completed in Exercise 42 in Stage 6.
6. Discuss the lists. Ask the participants what they learned about their attitudes and behaviors. Participants can then complete the first three columns outside the workshop.

1. This exercise can also be expanded into a journal. Have participants list their positive attitudes about being anti-racist. Have them record for one week their behaviors that are consistent with that attitude and those that are inconsistent. This activity helps participants see the gaps between behavior and attitude for themselves and will help them recognize their individual racism. **Note to Facilitator**
2. It is important to emphasize that this exercise focuses on positive anti-racist attitudes. It may also be necessary to explain how often people act on their racist attitudes in a similar manner. This exercise can be adapted for that goal as well.
3. The exercise leads into Stage 6, in which participants will be developing specific action strategies to combat racism.

25 minutes **Time**

178

Stage 6   Developing Action Strategies

Introduction

This training program and the theory behind it are directed toward this final stage. Unless this stage is achieved, little has been accomplished. Stage 6 concentrates on defining and developing action strategies to address racism. The goal is to move participants to becoming "anti-racist racists." To help reach this goal, the exercises in this stage are designed to

1. Help participants explore specific action strategies.
2. Help participants define and develop a specific course of action to combat racism.
3. Help participants develop an ongoing support base.
4. Help participants name the next steps for their continued exploration of personal racism.

Rationale

In this last stage one clear objective must be met if the training program is to be successful: participants must leave it willing and ready to take action against racism. This phase is called "becoming an anti-racist racist." Anti-racist racists are white people who understand their racism and accept that given the dynamics of racism in the United States today, they will always be racist but take action to actively challenge it in situations where they have some power. In other words, anti-racist racists take action to try to solve the white problem. The most important point of this training program is that *inaction is racism.* We whites must not only understand racism—how it developed and how it operates in our society and in our personal lives—but *do* something with that knowledge that will effect change in our racist system. That is the essence of the last stage—and the purpose of the entire training program. Otherwise we have colluded and merely served to create more knowledgeable racists.

You must help participants meet the challenge of taking action to challenge racism by focusing on the costs and benefits of taking such action. Participants must explore what's in it for them, including the risks and the benefits. Once participants understand the price they pay

179

either for action or for inaction, they can explore possible action projects. They must be willing to make a commitment to specific action. Once that commitment is made, the initial steps must be defined so that participants have a clear direction about how to begin. A vital part of this process includes the development of a support base. Often the workshop group itself serves this function.

The second important goal of this final stage is to assure that when the participants end the formal workshop experience, their personal exploration of racism will not end. Racism is so deeply ingrained in us that clearly one workshop cannot uncover all its aspects, or teach us all that there is to know about it. Participants must leave with the task of continuing to learn about racism on all levels. Stage 6 is designed to help participants name their next steps in that exploration. These steps may include reading more about the subject, taking a course on one aspect of the workshop, or participating in an interracial group in which they can deepen their knowledge and partner with people of color for change. The important thing participants must understand is that racism is not easily solved or even identified. A commitment of time and energy is necessary if one is truly committed to becoming an anti-racist.

Method

In this last stage you have one basic task: to make certain that all participants are clear on their goals and actions for the future. You can help participants develop their goals by breaking down some of the possible action projects into clear and specific steps. Participants need to understand that their actions need not be grand gestures and that they should start with a reachable goal. Clearly they can change neither themselves nor the system overnight. Often participants feel overwhelmed at the scope of racism and do not know where to begin. One way you can help in this process is to inform the participants about specific activities that are already under way in their community. This information may help the participants become involved and also can provide an established support base. To encourage the participants to explore their personal racism further, share your knowledge of specific resources that can give participants a clear direction. These resources may include other workshops, materials, books, records, resource people, and courses.

Make the group aware that the end of the workshop marks not the end of a process but the beginning. If the participants fail to take action

180

on what they have learned, they have not moved at all. If they commit themselves to take action and meet that commitment, they are beginning the long, sometimes hard road to liberation. The challenge to you as a facilitator is to impress this point on all the participants.

Exercise 42   Developing Action on Personal Inconsistencies

Goals
1. To help participants develop action strategies that will close the gaps between the inconsistencies in their attitudes and their behavior.
2. To help participants define their next steps in their exploration of personal racism.

Materials Needed

Sheets developed in Exercise 41, "Discovering Inconsistencies between Attitudes and Behavior"

Pens and pencils

Instructions
1. Participants should have the sheets they began in Exercise 41.
2. Ask them to title Column IV "Actions I Can Take" and then list things they can do to make their behavior more consistent with their attitudes, or further actions they can take to better support their anti-racist attitudes.
3. Have them share their lists with the group.
4. Ask them to star one action on the list that they *want* to take.

Note to Facilitator

This exercise helps participants define some actions they can take to counter their personal racism. They should be encouraged to consider not only direct but also indirect forms of action. Indirect action may include finding ways to learn more about one's racism and its dynamics, asking someone to serve as a process observer and give feedback about how consistent their behavior is with their attitudes, or keeping a journal of behavior and reviewing it weekly for consistency and regular development of possible actions.

Time

40 minutes

Exercise 43   Fighting Racism: Personal Commitment

1. To assess participants' commitment to challenge and confront racism.   **Goals**
2. To help participants generate ideas about actions they can take.

Copies of "Self-Assessment of Anti-Racist Behaviors" (p. 184)   **Materials**
Copies of "Commitment to Combat Racism" (p. 186)   **Needed**
Pens and pencils

1. Hand out copies of "Self-Assessment of Anti-Racist Behaviors."   **Instructions**
2. Ask participants to check those items on which they have taken action.
3. Ask them to share their lists.
4. Discuss the following:
   a. Reactions to the list and the items.
   b. The kinds of actions that can be taken on institutional and personal levels.
5. Hand out copies of "Commitment to Combat Racism." Brainstorm additional kinds of actions that can be taken.

1. At the start of this exercise participants may feel burdened by the   **Note to**
   commitment to action. This exercise should help them realize that   **Facilitator**
   they can take action on various levels and in various ways. They gain
   a sense of support when they understand that they do not have to
   do something grandiose or take on a whole system in order to begin
   actively challenging racism.
2. "Commitment to Combat Racism" lists action strategies that were
   developed for a general audience. They can be adapted for specific
   systems and institutions. Encourage the participants to modify the list
   to fit their own setting.

30 minutes   **Time**

183

Self-Assessment of Anti-Racist Behavior

Check the appropriate column to indicate whether you have taken action on the items listed below.

Question	Yes	No
1. I educate myself about the culture and experience of other social identity groups—including blacks, Asian Americans, Latinas/Latinos, and Native Americans—by actively attending classes, workshops, cultural events, reading, talking to people, and so forth.		
2. I spend time reflecting on my own childhood to analyze where and how I received racist messages.		
3. I look at my own attitudes and behaviors as a young adult to determine how I am colluding with racism in this society.		
4. I evaluate my own use of language to see if I am using terms or phrases that are subtly racist or reinforce unequal status between blacks and whites.		
5. I avoid stereotyping and generalizing about people based on their race.		
6. I value cultural differences and avoid statements such as "I never think of you as black," which discredits human differences and cultural heritage.		
7. I am aware of and can explore and discuss with comfort diversity issues, including racism.		
8. I am open to having others point out ways in which my behavior may be racist or colludes with racism.		

Question	Yes	No
9. I am comfortable interacting honestly with someone of another race and willing to discuss issues of racism with her or him.		
10. I consciously monitor TV programs, newspapers, and advertising for racist content.		
11. I feel free to ask people who are using racist language and behavior to refrain from doing so in my presence and am comfortable stating my reasons.		
12. I am willing to be active in my school, workplace, and community to achieve inclusive and anti-racist environments.		
13. I actively support anti-racist political action by campaigning for anti-racist candidates, participating in letter writing and other political efforts, and supporting anti-racist legislation.		
14. I am satisfied with my current level of actions in challenging racism.		

Commitment to Combat Racism

1. Educating family members and close friends.
2. Raising issues with colleagues at work.
3. Providing information services to social and religious groups, by bringing in speakers, putting up posters, recommending books, suggesting workshops, and so on.
4. Acting as a referral resource—directing whites to people or groups who might be of assistance.
5. Acting as a race role model, questioning the white power structure.
6. Establishing discussion groups, colloquia, and so on.
7. Finding resources (e.g., films, videos, Web sites, books) that expose white racism and develop new strategies for whites to help challenge and address racism.
8. Becoming politically active in the fight against racism by writing elected officials, supporting anti-racism candidates, working for anti-racism legislation, and so on.
9. Working with other whites who are genuinely interested in making sense of racial issues and becoming anti-racist.
10. Speaking up when seeing behaviors or hearing statements that are racist.
11. Actively examining the privileges that whites receive and the disparate treatment of people of color.
12. Partnering with people of color as an ally for change.

Exercise 44   The Costs and Benefits of Dealing
with Racism

1. To help participants explore their motives for becoming anti-racist racists.
2. To help participants explore the price they pay for being racist and/or becoming anti-racist racists.

Copies of "What Would I Give Up by Acting against Racism?" (p. 189)
Pens and pencils

1. Hand out the sheet "What Would I Give Up by Acting against Racism?"
2. Ask the participants to fill out the sheet and to be as honest as possible.
3. Discuss the responses and reactions.

1. This sheet focuses on participants' real motives for dealing with racism. It is especially important to spend time processing question 6, which highlights people's motives for becoming anti-racist racists. It is also important to make sure that participants are honest with themselves and the group about the prices they are paying for being racists. Sometimes participants respond with the answer they feel is "correct," rather than what they are really feeling. Part of your responsibility in this exercise is to get to those real feelings.
2. This exercise helps participants get in touch with the realities of taking action steps so that they are clear about why they want to do so. You must help them explore their motives and reasons for wanting to take action. Some people may still be feeling that they want to "help" people of color. This is paternalistic racism similar to the kind found in Exercise 37, "After You, My Dear Alphonse." It is crucial that participants really understand the assumption that racism is a white problem. It may be helpful to ask them to fantasize the rewards they expect to gain from taking action. If they seem to expect thanks or

gratitude from people of color, they are engaging in paternalistic racism, similar to the kind reflected in Exercise 37 and Exercise 40.

3. It is crucial that participants honestly find what's in it for them. Self-interest is a key to combating racism. Individuals must identify both the cost of not addressing racism and the opportunity that exists if they do. Similarly, in working for change within organizations, it is essential that one identify the self-interest of the system—what's in it for the system to be different—as a motivator for real change.

Time   25 minutes

What Would I Give Up by Acting against Racism?

1. What would I give up by acting against racism?

2. How am I benefiting from racism?

3. What price am I paying for my racism?

4. What is my worst fantasy of what could happen if people of color were now in power?

5. What limits do I put on helping change and addressing institutional racism?

6. What needs of my own would I satisfy by being actively anti-racist?

Exercise 45   Dealing with Racism: Role-plays

Goals

1. To have participants develop alternative mechanisms and tools to deal with racist situations.
2. To have participants role-play some of these alternatives that they can later use in real-life situations.

Materials Needed

Paper
Pens and pencils

Instructions

1. Ask participants to write down a racist situation that they have had to deal with. Have them explain on paper each person's position in the situation.
2. Collect and shuffle the papers. Ask for volunteers to role-play the situations.
3. Have group members enact the role-playing. Process with the group and look at alternative actions.
4. Repeat the process.

Note to Facilitator

This exercise is helpful in bringing participants into the framework of their real-life situations. It is also helpful in giving them real and specific alternative actions that they can take.

Time

10 to 15 minutes per role-play

Exercise 46   Strategy and Action Planning

1. To help participants define and develop a specific action plan to deal with racism on the individual level. **Goals**
2. To help participants define and develop a specific action plan to deal with racism in their environment.

Sheets from Exercises 42 and 43 **Materials**
Copies of Strategy and Action Plan (two per person) (p. 193) **Needed**

1. Have the participants reread their sheets from Exercises 42 and 43. **Instructions**
2. Have them individually pick out at least one personal issue from Exercise 42 that they would like to explore further and from Exercise 43 at least one action they can take to make changes in their environment.
3. Hand out two copies of the Strategy and Action Plan to each person. Ask the participants to fill out one copy for their personal objective and one for their institutional objective.
4. Have the participants share their projects. You may want to encourage people to partner with each other on their institutional projects. This creates a support system and encourages cooperation.
5. Ask the participants to list the next steps they must take to meet their objectives.
6. Have them share their next steps with the group. As part of this process, ask them to share how they can support one another.

1. It is essential that participants be as clear as possible about their goals and their course of action, that is, the next steps to take. Your role is to help participants be as specific as possible in developing their project forms. **Note to Facilitator**
2. It is also important to stress the need for a support system. The members of the group must be able to identify their resources and partners. Process this carefully when going over the Strategy and Action Plan.

3. It is important to point out that participants must not take action in a vacuum. That is, they must be clear about whose needs they are trying to respond to. If, for example, one person's goal is to ensure that legislators are responding to the needs of people of color, that participant must have some steps in the plan that allow her or him to learn what those needs are. Again, whites' efforts to "help" people of color are often forms of paternalism, not positive action. In dealing with *white* racism, action must be taken to deal with *white* people. And if actions are taken with respect to people of color, they must be taken in partnership *with* people of color, not *for* them.
4. You should stress criteria for success and evaluation. One way to assess one's success is to set up a timeline and try to accomplish specific steps in a certain period. Sometimes suggesting that the group meet again in about a month to assess how well they have met their stated objectives is useful in helping them get started on taking some action.
5. Above all, remember that *inaction is racism.*

Time   1 hour

192

Strategy and Action Plan

1. Identify the problem you want to resolve.

2. What are your *specific* goals?

3. Achieving this goal will fulfill what personal needs?

4. What risks are involved? Are they worth it?

5. What resources (people, support, materials) do you need to help achieve this goal? How will these resources be acquired?

6. What power and influence (formal or informal) do you have to reach this goal? (Include people who are important to the change effort.)

7. What resistance may you encounter? How can you decrease it?

8. What support do you have? How can you increase it?

9. What is the potential for success? What criteria will you use to evaluate your success?

10. What next steps must you take to meet this goal? Be specific.

Exercise 47   Evaluation and Feedback

Goals
1. To obtain feedback from participants on your effectiveness as the facilitator.
2. To obtain feedback and an evaluation of the strengths and weaknesses of the workshop design.

Materials Needed
Copies of Feedback Sheet (p. 195)
Pens and pencils

Instructions
1. Hand out copies of the Feedback Sheet.
2. Ask the participants to fill it out as honestly and as specifically as possible.
3. Ask them to share with the group their feelings—positive or negative—about the workshop itself and your role as the facilitator.

Note to Facilitator
1. This sheet helps you gain a better idea of your strengths and weaknesses.
2. It is not necessary for the participants to share their comments with the group. Some participants do not want to disclose what they have written, and this preference should be honored. Participants will usually share general feelings with the group. The more specific data come in the answers on the sheets.

Time
20 minutes

Feedback Sheet: Course and Facilitator Evaluation

1. How helpful has this workshop been for you?

Not at all helpful				Somewhat helpful					Very helpful	
0	1	2	3	4	5	6	7	8	9	10

2. Identify one thing you did to facilitate your learning.

3. Identify two key things you will take away from this experience.

4. List the elements (resources, exercises, etc.) that you feel were the most helpful to you. Why were they helpful?

5. List the elements that you feel were the least helpful. Why?

6. What changes would you recommend to improve this program?

7. How would you rate your facilitator?

Not at all effective				Somewhat effective					Highly effective	
0	1	2	3	4	5	6	7	8	9	10

Why?

8. Additional comments:

Exercise 48   Closing

Goals
1. To bring the workshop to a close.
2. To leave participants thinking about their experience in the workshop as they say good-bye.

Materials Needed

CD/cassette player
Appropriate music selection. Some possibilities include

- "The World Is a Ghetto" by War
- "What's Goin' On" by Marvin Gaye
- "Visions," "Living for the City," "Higher Ground," "You Haven't Done Nothing," "Love's in Need of Love Today" by Stevie Wonder
- "The Way It Is" by Bruce Hornsby & The Range
- "Someday We'll All Be Free" by Donny Hathaway
- "Tennessee" by Arrested Development
- "A Change Is Gonna Come" by Sam Cooke (versions also available by Otis Redding, Aretha Franklin, and others)

OR:
Getting Along (video)
TV
VCR

Instructions
1. It is time to end the workshop. One way to close is to use a music selection that ties in some of the many issues with which the group has been struggling over the course of the workshop. Several possibilities appear in the list above. They can be played as the final group experience.
2. An alternative is to show the video *Getting Along*, which provides an upbeat, positive message with which to end the session.

196

Feel free to adapt this closing exercise in any way you think is appropriate, including allowing each participant to express to the group what she or he learned and her or his overall reactions and feelings. **Note to Facilitator**

Varies **Time**

References

Adams, P. (1973). *Attitude exploration survey.* Amherst, MA: University of Massachusetts, Center for Racial Understanding.

Allen, B. (1971). Implications of social reaction research for racism. *Psychological Reports, 29,* 883–91.

The American Heritage Dictionary of the English Language (4th ed.). (2000). New York: Houghton Mifflin Co.

Arrested Development (1992). Tennessee. On *3 Years, 5 Months & 2 Days in the Life of . . .* [CD]. Los Angeles, CA: Chrysalis.

Beck, J. (1973). *The counselor and black/white relations.* Boston: Houghton Mifflin.

Bennett, J. L. (1966). *Before the Mayflower: History of the Negro in America, 1619–1964.* New York: Macmillan.

Berry, W. (1970). *The hidden wound.* Boston: Houghton Mifflin.

Bidol, P. (1971). *Reflections of whiteness in a white racist society* [pamphlet]. Detroit: P.A.C.T.

Bidol, P. (1972). *Racism definition list.* Detroit: New Perspectives on Race.

Breitman, G. (Ed.). (1970). *By any means necessary: Speeches, interviews, and a letter by Malcolm X.* New York: Pathfinder.

Brookings Institution. (1999). *Race in America: New approaches to bridging the divide. A Brookings forum.* Washington, DC: Federal News Service, Inc.

Brown, R. L. (1972). Racism: Worst tool of cruelty. *Integrated Education, 10,* 3–10.

Carmichael S. & Hamilton, C. (1967). *Black power: Politics of liberation.* New York: Vintage.

Center for the Study of White American Culture. (1999). *Racial awareness quiz.* Roselle, NJ: Center for the Study of White American Culture.

Citron, A. (1969). *The rightness of whiteness: World of the white child in a segregated society.* [pamphlet]. Detroit: Ohio Regional Educational Lab.

Clark, K. (1963). *Prejudice and your child.* Boston: American.

Cleaver, E. (1968). *Soul on ice.* New York: Dell.

Cobbs, P. (1972). Ethnotherapy. *Intellectual Digest, 2,* 26–28.

Comer, J. (1991). White racism: Its root, form, and function. In R. L. Jones (Ed.), *Black Psychology* (pp. 591–96). Berkeley, CA: Cobb & Henry.

Cooke, S. (1986). A change is gonna come. On *The Man and His Music* [CD]. Nashville, TN: RCA.

Cross, W. E., Jr. (1971). Negro-to-black conversion experience. *Black World, 20,* 13–27.

Daniels, O. C. B. (1973). The relationship between interracial apperception and ideology. Ph.D. dissertation, University of Massachusetts.

Daniel, O. C. B. (1974). *Project RATE.* Amherst: University of Massachusetts, Student Affairs.

Davidson, A. (Producer/Director). (1990). *The Lunch Date* [Video]. (Available from Du Art Film and Video, 245 West 55th Street, New York, NY 10019, 1-212-757-4580, *www.duart.com.*)

Delaney, L. (1990). The other bodies in the river. In R. L. Jones (Ed.), *Black Psychology* (pp. 597–607). Berkeley, CA: Cobb & Henry.

Dixon, R. L. (2000). Racism has its privileges: A short treatise on why White privilege stands in the way of black progress. *The Black World Today* [On-line journal], Available FTP: *http://www.tbwt.com/views/feat/feat1781.asp.*

Du Bois, W. E. B. (1920). *Darkwater.* New York: Harcourt, Brace & Howe.

Du Bois, W. E. B. (1994). *Souls of black folk.* New York: Gramercy Books (orig. pub. 1903).

Edler, J. (1974). White on white: An anti-racism manual for white educators in the process of becoming. Ph.D. dissertation, University of Massachusetts.

Gaye, M. (1971). What's goin' on. On *What's Goin' On* [CD]. Detroit, MI: Tamla.

Goldin, P. (1970). Model for racial awareness training for teachers in integrated schools. *Integrated Education, 8,* 62–64.

Goodman, M. (1964). *Race awareness in young children.* New York: Collier.

Greenwald, H. J. & Oppenheim, D. B. (1968). Reported magnitude of self misidentification among Negro children. *Journal of Social Psychology, 8,* 49–52.

Gregory, D. (1997). *The Light Side: The Dark Side* [CD]. Ardmore, PA: Collectibles.

Hardiman, R. (1994). White racial identity development in the United States. In E. P. Salett & D. R. Koslow (Eds.), *Race, Ethnicity and Self: Identity in Multicultural Perspective* (pp. 117–40). Washington, DC: NMCI Publications.

Hathaway, D. (1973). Someday we'll all be free. On *Extension of a Man* [CD]. New York: Atco.

Helms, J. E. (1993). *Black and white racial identity: Theory, research and practice.* Westport, CT: Prager.

Hitchcock, J. (2002). *Lifting the White Veil.* Roselle, NJ: Crandall, Dostie & Douglass.

Hornsby, B. & the Range (1986). The way it is. On *The Way It Is* [CD]. Nashville, TN: RCA.

Jackson, B. (1976). Black identity development. In L. Golubschick and B. Persky (Eds.), *Urban and Social Education Issues* (pp. 158–64). Dubuque, IA: Kendall/Hunt.

Jackson, S. (1991). After you, my dear Alphonse. In Farrar, Straus & Giroux (Eds.), *The Lottery and Other Stories* (pp. 85–89). New York: Noonday Press.

Jensen, R. (1998, July 19). White privilege shapes the U.S. *Baltimore Sun,* p. C-1.

Jensen, R. (1999, July 4). More thoughts on why system of white privilege is wrong. *Baltimore Sun,* p. C-1.

Jones, J. (1972). *Prejudice and racism*. Reading, MA: Addison-Wesley.

Jordan, W. D. (1968). *White over black: American attitudes toward the Negro, 1550–1812*. Baltimore: Penguin.

Joyce, F. (n.d.). *An analysis of American racism* [pamphlet]. Somerville, MA: New England Free Press.

Katz, J. (1978). *White awareness: Handbook for anti-racism training*. Norman: University of Oklahoma Press.

Katz, J. & Ivey, A. (1977). White awareness: The frontier of racism awareness training. *Personnel and Guidance Journal, 55 (8)*, 485–89.

Katz, J. H. & Miller, F. A. (2002). *The inclusion breakthrough: Unleashing the real power of diversity*. San Francisco, CA: Berrett-Koehler.

Katz, J. H. & Miller, F. A. (1995) *Cultural diversity as a development process: The path from monocultural club to an inclusive workplace*. New York: Pfeiffer and Company.

Kerner Commission. (1968). *Report of the National Advisory Commission on Civil Disorders*. Washington, DC: U.S. Government Printing Office.

Kivel, P. (1995). *Uprooting racism: How white people can work for racial justice*. Philadelphia, PA: New Society Publishers.

Knowles L. & Prewitt, K. (Eds.) (1969). *Institutional racism in America*. Englewood Cliffs, NJ: Prentice-Hall.

Kovel, J. (1970). *White racism: A psychohistory*. New York: Pantheon.

Kranz, P. L. (1972). Racial confrontation group implemented within a junior college. *Negro Educational Review, 23*, 70–80.

Lacy, D. (1972). *White use of blacks*. New York: McGraw-Hill.

Larkin, W. & Walker, M. (1994). *Internalized dominance and workplace dynamics* [Workshop handout]. Washington, DC: National Multicultural Institute.

Luckasiewicz, M. & Harvey, E. (Producers). (1991). *True colors* [Video]. (Available from Trainer's Toolchest, 403 Gardenia Lane, Buffalo Grave, IL 60089. 1-877-288-6657, *www.trainerstoolchest.com*.)

Marrow, A. J. (1967). Events leading to the establishment of the National Training Laboratories. *Journal of Applied Behavioral Science, 3*, 144–50.

McIntosh, P. (1988). White privilege: Unpacking the invisible knapsack. In *White privilege and male privilege: A personal account of coming to see correspondences through work in Women's Studies*. (Working Paper No. 189.) Wellesley, MA: Wellesley College Center for Research on Women.

Moore, R. (1973). A rationale, description, and analysis of a racism awareness program for white teachers. Ph.D. dissertation, University of Massachusetts.

Morland, J. (1962). Racial acceptance and preference of nursery school children in a southern city. *Merrill-Palmer Quarterly, 8*, 372–80.

Myrdal, G. (1944). *An American dilemma*. (Vols. 1 & 2). New York: Harper and Row.

Peters, W. (1970). *The Eye of the Storm* [Video]. (Available from Trainer's Toolchest, 403 Gardenia Lane, Buffalo Grave, IL 60089. 1-877-288-6657, *www.trainerstoolchest.com*.)

Pinderhughes, E. (1989). *Understanding race, ethnicity, and power: The key to efficacy in clinical practice*. New York: Free Press.

President's Initiative on Race. (1998). *One America in the 21st Century: Forging a new future; The Advisory Board reports to the President*. (DHHS Publication No. 98-0206.) Washington, DC: U.S. Government Printing Office.

Quarles, B. (1964). *The Negro in the making of America*. New York: Collier.

Riggs, M. (Director/Writer/Producer). (1987). *Ethnic Notions* [Video]. (Available from California Newsreel, PO Box 2284, South Burlington, VT 05407. 1-877-811-7495, *www.newsreel.org*.)

Roberts, D. (1975). The treatment of cultural scripts. *Transactional Analysis Journal, 5, (1)*, 29–35.

Robinson, R. & Spaights, E. (1969). Study of attitudinal change through lecture discussion workshop. *Adult Education, 19*, 163–71.

Rubin, I. (1967). The reduction of prejudice through laboratory training. *Journal of Applied Behavioral Science, 3*, 29–51.

Sainte-Marie, B. (1990). *The Best of Buffy Sainte-Marie* (CD). Santa Monica, CA: Vanguard Records.

Sargent, A. (1977). *Beyond sex roles*. St. Paul, MN: West Publishing Company.

Schwartz, B. & Disch, R. (Eds.) (1970). *White racism: Its history, pathology, and practice*. New York: Dell.

Singh, J. & Yancey, A. (1974). Racial attitudes in white first grade children. *Journal of Educational Research, 67*, 370–72.

Steckler, G. (1957). Authoritarian ideology in Negro college students. *Journal of Abnormal Social Psychology, 54*, 396-99.

Steinberg, D. (n.d.). *Racism in America: Definition and analysis* (pamphlet). Detroit, MI: P.A.C.T.

Terry, R. (1970). *For whites only*. Grand Rapids, MI: Eerdmans.

Thandeka. (1999). *Learning to be white: Money, race, and God in America*. New York: Continuum.

Thiederman, S. (Producer). (1996). *Getting Along* [Video]. (Available from Cross-Cultural Communications, 4585 48th Street, San Diego, CA 92115. 1-619-583-4478, *www.thiederman.com*.)

Thomas, A. & Sillen, S. (1972). *Racism and psychiatry*. New York: Brunner-Mazel.

Thomas, C. W. (1971). *Boys no more: A black psychologist's view of community*. Beverly Hills, CA: Glencoe.

Timmel, S. (n.d.). *White on white: A handbook for groups working against racism*. Cambridge, MA: Robinson and Richardson.

Uhlemann, M. (1968). Behavioral change outcomes and marathon group therapy. Master's thesis, Colorado State University.

United States Commission on Civil Rights. (1970). *Racism in America and how to combat it*. (Publication No. 0-357-458.) Washington, DC: U.S. Government Printing Office.

Wah, L. M. (Producer/Director) & Hunter, M. (Producer). (1994). *The Color of Fear* [Video]. (Available from Stirfry Productions, 15th Santa Clara Avenue, Oakland, CA 94610. 1-510-420-8292, *www.stirfryseminars.com.*)

Walker, J. & Hamilton, L. (1973). A Chicano/black/white encounter. *Personnel and Guidance Journal, 51,* 471–77.

War (1972). The world is a ghetto. On *The World Is a Ghetto* (CD). New York: United Artists.

Welsing, F. C. (1970). *Cress theory of color confrontation.* Washington, DC: Howard University.

Wilkinson, C. B. (1973). Problems in black-white encounter groups. *International Journal of Group Psychotherapy, 23,* 155–65.

Winter, S. K. (1971). Black man's bluff. *Psychology Today, 5,* 39–43, 78–81.

Wonder, S. (1973). Higher ground. On *Innervisions* (CD). Detroit, MI: Tamla.

Wonder, S. (1973). Living for the city. On *Innervisions* (CD). Detroit, MI: Tamla.

Wonder, S. (1973). Visions. On *Innervisions* (CD). Detroit, MI: Tamla.

Wonder, S. (1974). You haven't done nothing. On *Fulfillingness' First Finale* (CD). Detroit, MI: Tamla.

Wonder, S. (1976). Love's in need of love today. On *Songs in the Key of Life* (CD). Detroit, MI: Tamla.

Young, W. (1970) Exceptional children. Speech presented at Council for Exceptional Children, Reston, VA.

Additional Resources and Readings

Web Sites

About.com Race Relations Forum
http://racerelations.about.com/newsissues/racerelations/mbody.htm

American Truths
http://www.americantruths.com/

Anti-Racist Action
http://www.aranet.org/

AntiRacismNet
http://www.igc.org/igc/gateway/arnindex.html

antiracist.com
http://www.antiracist.com/frameset.htm

Applied Research Center (*ColorLines Magazine* is on this site)
http://www.arc.org/

The Atlantic Online—November 1993: Reverse Racism, or How the Pot Got to
    Call the Kettle Black
http://www.theatlantic.com/politics/race/fish.htm

Beyond Prejudice
http://www.eburg.com/beyond.prejudice/

Birthrights Magazine
http://www.birthrights.org

The Catholic Mobile Racial Justice Page
http://www.mcgill.pvt.k12.al.us/jerryd/cm/race.htm

Center for the Study of White American Culture, Inc.
http://www.euroamerican.org

Civilrights.org
http://www.civilrights.org

Crosspoint Anti Racism
http://www.antiracisme.nl/crosspoint/

Educational Justice
http://www.edjustice.org/

facing history and ourselves
http://www.facing.org/facing/fhao2.nsf/main/about+us?opendocument

204

Fisk Race Relations Institute
http://www.fiskrri.org/

Implicit Association Test
http://buster.cs.yale.edu/implicit/

infoplease.com – definition of racism
http://www.infoplease.com/ipd/A0614344.html

Institute for the Study of Academic Racism
http://www.ferris.edu/htmls/OTHERSRV/ISAR/homepage.htm

League of United Latin American Citizens
http://www.lulac.org/Welcome.html

(American Indian) MASCOTS – Racism in Schools by State
http://www.aics.org/mascot/mascot.html

Media Action Network for Asian Americans
http://janet.org/~manaa/

NAACP Online
http://www.naacp.org/

National Association of Black and White Men together
http://www.nabwmt.com/

The National Coalition Building Institute
http://www.ncbi.org/

National Coalition on Racism in Sports and the Media
http://www.aics.org/NCRSM/index.htm

National Conference for Community and Justice
http://www.nccj.org/nccj3.nsf/?Open

National Council of La Raza
http://www.nclr.org/

National Resource Center for the Healing of Racism
http://www.ntlhealingracism.org/

National Urban League
http://www.nul.org/

California News Reel
www.newsreel.org

The People's Institute for Survival and Beyond
http://www.peoplesinstitute.org/peoplesinstitute/index.html

Race, Racism, and the Law
http://www.udayton.edu/~race/

Recovering Racists Network
http://www.jmckenzie.com/rrn/

Say NO to Racism!
http://www.gov.nb.ca/hrc-cdp/e/sayno.htm

Sojourners Magazine (Christian faith-based)
http://www.sojo.net/index.cfm

Southern Poverty Law Center
http://www.splcenter.org/

Tolerance.org
http://www.tolerance.org/index.jsp

Viewing Race
http://www.viewingrace.org/project/index.html

Organizations without Web Sites

Crossroads Ministry
425 South Central Park Avenue
Chicago, IL 60624
773.638.0166

Study Guides

Resisting racism: An action guide
Edited by Gerald L. Mallon, Ed.D.
Published by the National Association of Black and White Men Together.
http://www.nabwmt.com/racism.html
Challenging White supremacy: America's original sin. A study guide on white
racism. New and expanded edition.
Sojourners (see Web site)
http://www.sojo.net/resources/index.cfm/cfid/75605/cftoken/9262184/mode/di
splay_detail/ResourceID/104/action/catalog.html

Video

A Class Divided
Documents a reunion of Iowa teacher Jane Elliott and her third-grade class of
1970, subjects of an ABC News television documentary entitled *The Eye of
the Storm.* Shows how her experimental curriculum on the evils of discrim-
ination had a lasting effect on the lives of the students.
Producer: Yale University Films for Frontline; produced for the Documentary
Consortium by WGBH Boston.
Year: 1986
Length: 57 minutes
Distributor: PBS Video
Washington, DC

Workshops (appearing regularly)

White Racial Awareness Program—Los Angeles Chapter, NCCJ

206

Challenging White Supremacy—Tides Foundation, San Francisco

White People Working on Racism—Training for Change, Philadelphia

What White People Can Do About Racism—The Kaleel Jamison Consulting Group, Inc., various locations

Books and Articles (Print)

Barndt, J. (1991). *Dismantling racism: The continuing challenge to white America*. Minneapolis, MN: Augsburg Fortress.

Battle, P. C., Ph.D. & Battle, K. P., M.S. (2001). *Pigmentocracy: How words create, perpetuate, and sustain it*. Burtonsville, MD: Pat Battle & Associates.

Berger, M. (1999). *White lies: Race and the myths of whiteness*. New York: Farrar, Straus and Giroux.

Chisom, R. & Washington, M. (1997). *Undoing racism: A philosophy of international social change*. New Orleans, LA: People's Institute Press.

Delgado, R. & Stefancic, J. (1997). *Critical white studies: Looking behind the mirror*. Philadelphia, PA: Temple University Press.

Derman-Sparks, L. & Phillips, C. B. (1997). *Teaching/learning anti-racism: A developmental approach*. New York: Teachers College Press (Columbia Univ.).

Feagin, J. R. & Hernán, V. (1995). *White racism: The basics*. New York: Routledge.

Helms, J. E. (1992). *A race is a nice thing to have: A guide to being a white person or understanding the white persons in your life*. Topeka, KA: Content Communications.

Hitchcock, J. & Flint, C. (1997, February). Decentering whiteness. *The WHITENESS PAPERS, No. 1*. Roselle, NJ: Center for the Study of White American Culture.

Holladay, J. R. (2000, November). White antiracist activism: A personal roadmap. *The WHITENESS PAPERS, No. 4*. Roselle, NJ: Center for the Study of White American Culture.

Ignatiev, N. (1995). *How the Irish became white*. New York: Routledge.

Johnson, A. G. (2001). *Privilege, power and difference*. Mountain View, CA: Mayfield Publishing Company.

Katz, J. H. (1999, December). White culture and racism: Working for organizational change in the United States. *The WHITENESS PAPERS, No. 3*. Roselle, NJ: Center for the Study of White American Culture.

Kochman, T. (1981). *Black and white styles in conflict*. Chicago, IL: University of Chicago Press.

Loewen, J. W. (1995). *Lies my teacher told me: Everything your American history textbook got wrong*. New York: Touchstone.

Morrison, T. (1992). *Playing in the dark: Whiteness and the literary imagination*. New York: Vintage Books.

The National Conference for Community and Justice. (1998). *Intergroup relations in the United States: Programs and organizations*. New York: National Conference for Community and Justice.

Ponterotto, J. G. & Pedersen, P. B. (1993). *Preventing prejudice: A guide for counselors and educators*. Newbury Park, CA: Sage.

Rutstein, N. (1993). *Healing racism in America: A prescription for the disease*. Springfield, MA: Whitcomb Publishing.

Shearer, J. M. (1994). *Enter the river: Healing steps from white privilege toward racial reconciliation*. Scottsdale, PA: Herald Press.

Stalvey, L. M. (1989). *The education of a WASP*. Madison: University of Wisconsin Press (orig. pub. 1970).

Tatum, B. D. (1997). *"Why are all the black kids sitting together in the cafeteria?" and other conversations about race*. New York: Basic Books.

Thompson, C. (1997, October). White men and the denial of racism. *The WHITE-NESS PAPERS, No. 2.* Roselle, NJ: Center for the Study of White American Culture.

Thompson, L. (n.d.). *WHITEFOLKS funnies*. Self-published.

Wellman, D. T. (1993). *Portraits of white racism* (2d ed.). New York: Cambridge University Press.

Index

White-awareness training. *See* White-on-white workshop

White culture, 18, 21, 22, 56

White identity development, 22

White-on-white workshop, 23; assumptions of, 25–28; content and process, 28; exercises, 28, 31; facilitator in, 5, 27–32; flexibility and adaptability of, 5, 30; formats, 28–29, 31–32; groups, 29; measuring effectiveness of, 5, 23, 32; objectives and goals, 24–25; stages of, 25, 28–29. *See also* Workshop (stages)

White privilege, 10–11, 18

White racism, 25, 28, 56, 63, 83; cultural, 121–44; effects of, 7–8, 24; historical, 8; ideologies, 26, 62; institutional, 10, 17, 24, 27, 55; personal, 121, 147–77; power of, 63; racial myths, 5; strategies for change, 25, 26. *See also* Racism

Whites, 3, 19, 123, 128–29; attitudes of, 4, 5, 21, 25, 26, 103, 182; behaviors of, 5, 24–25, 32, 182; being white, 14, 16, 22, 24, 28; discrepancies of, 24; effects of racism on, 5, 8, 11–18, 24, 55; fears of, 25, 26, 29, 104, 107–108; guilt feeling of, 15, 22, 24, 29, 56; history, 20, 21; racial myths, 5, 107–108, 167; reeducation of, 18, 24, 26, 103; superiority attitudes, 10–12, 14–17, 23; training programs for, 3, 5, 24–33

Women's equality, 3

Women's Movement, 27

Workshop:

STAGE 1: concentric-circles exercise in, 41–42; definition of prejudice in, 43–44; definition of racism in, 51–52; designing a racist community in, 47–49; facilitator,

40, 48–49, 52; fuzzy concept exercise in, 50; *The Lunch Date* (video), 46; method of, 38–39; "Mini-Lecture on the Difference Between Prejudice and Racism" in, 44; objectives and goals of, 37–38, 40, 41, 43, 46, 47, 50, 51; Prejudice Definition Sheet in, 45; Racism Definition Sheet in, 53; "Racism Is . . . " sheet in, 48; STAGE 2: *The Best of Buffy St. Marie* (CD or cassette), 79; *The Color of Fear* (video), 92–93; "The Drawbridge" (story), 72–74; *Ethnic Notions* (video), 75–76; facilitator, 60, 61, 64–66, 73, 76, 78–80, 82, 84, 92–94; ideologies and slogans, 62; inconsistencies, 61; institutional racism, 83–84, 87–91; institutional racism and Native Americans, 79–80; institutional racism debate, 81–82; "Inventory of Racism" in, 87–91; *The Light Side, The Dark Side* (CD or cassette), 83; method of, 56; "Mini-Lecture, Kinds and Levels of Racism" in, 57–60; objectives and goals of, 55–57, 61, 63, 65, 72, 75, 77, 79, 81, 83, 85, 92, 94; power of institutional racism, 77–78; Racial Awareness Quiz, 94–100; racism in institutions, 86; "Racism Is . . . " sheet in, 61; rationale of, 55–56; Simulation Design 1, College Setting in, 67–68; Simulation Design 2, Public School Setting in, 69–71; simulation experience in, 65–66; simulation game in, 63–64; *True Colors* (video), 85; STAGE 3: Circle Break-in Exercise in, 109–10; facilitator, 106, 107, 110, 111, 115; "Fantasy, Bus Trip" in, 111, 113; fears about racism,